# THE OLD BRIDGE

# THE OLD BRIDGE

## CHRISTOPHER MERRILL

## THE THIRD BALKAN WAR AND THE AGE OF THE REFUGEE

MILKWEED
EDITIONS

Published 1995 by Milkweed Editions

Distributed by Publishers Group West

Printed in the United States of America

The maps on pages viii and ix are adapted from Zlatko Dizdarević, *Sarajevo: A War Journal* (New York: Fromm International, 1993). Reprinted with permission.
Cover design by Sally Wagner.
Cover art by Tomislav Kizman.
Interior design by Will Powers. The text of this book is set in Minion.

95  96  97  98  99      5  4  3  2  1

*First Edition*

Milkweed Editions is a not-for-profit publisher. We gratefully acknowledge support from the Bush Foundation, Target Stores, Dayton's, and Mervyn's by the Dayton Hudson Foundation; Ecolab Foundation; General Mills Foundation; Honeywell Foundation; Jerome Foundation; John S. and James L. Knight Foundation; The McKnight Foundation; Andrew W. Mellon Foundation; Minnesota State Arts Board through an appropriation by the Minnesota State Legislature; Challenge and Literature Programs of the National Endowment for the Arts; I. A. O'Shaughnessy Foundation; Piper Jaffray Companies, Inc.; John and Beverly Rollwagen Fund of the Minneapolis Foundation; The St. Paul Companies, Inc.; Star Tribune/ Cowles Media Foundation; Surdna Foundation; James R. Thorpe Foundation; Lila Wallace-Reader's Digest Literary Publishers Marketing Development Program, funded through a grant to the Council of Literary Magazines and Presses; and generous individuals.

Library of Congress Cataloging-in-Publication Data

Merrill, Christopher.
    The old bridge : the third Balkan War and the age of the refugee / Christopher Merrill. — 1st ed.
      p.   cm.
    ISBN 1-57131-208-0 (alk. paper)
    1. Yugoslav War, 1991–  — Refugees.   2. Yugoslav War, 1991–
— Personal narratives.   3. Forced migration — Yugoslavia — History
— 20th century.   I. Title.
    DR1313.7.R43M467   1995
    949.702′4—dc20                                              95–20061
                                                                CIP

This book is printed on acid-free paper.

*for Agha Shahid Ali*

ACKNOWLEDGEMENTS

The author would like to thank the following individuals without whose help and inspiration this book could not have been written: Agha Shahid Ali, Emilie Buchwald, Frederick Cuny, Mary Jo Cuny, Aleš Debeljak, Ferida Duraković, Lisa Gowdy-Merrill, Elizabeth Grossman, Peter Hadji-Ristic, Metka Krašovec, Elaine Lamattina, Dennis Maloney, Kent Morris, Nicholas Morris, Lynne Partington, Jadranka and Marina Pintarić, Albert and April Reda, Pat Reed, Tomaž Šalamun, Jim Schley, Amela and Goran Simić, Greg Simon, William Strachan, Mike Tharp, and Frederick Turner.

*Doors open on the sands, doors open on exile*
ST.-JOHN PERSE

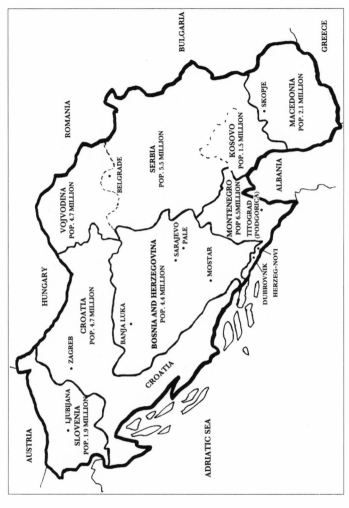

AUSTRIA

HUNGARY

ROMANIA

BULGARIA

GREECE

• LJUBLJANA
SLOVENIA
POP. 1.9 MILLION

• ZAGREB

CROATIA
POP. 4.7 MILLION

BANJA LUKA

VOJVODINA
POP. 4.7 MILLION

• BELGRADE

SERBIA
POP. 5.5 MILLION

KOSOVO
POP. 1.5 MILLION

• SKOPJE

MACEDONIA
POP. 2.1 MILLION

ALBANIA

BOSNIA AND HERZEGOVINA
POP. 4.4 MILLION

• SARAJEVO
• PALE

• MOSTAR

MONTENEGRO
POP. 6.5MILLION
TITOGRAD
(PODGORICA)

CROATIA

DUBROVNIK

HERZEG-NOVI

ADRIATIC SEA

YUGOSLAVIA BEFORE THE WAR

**Occupied by the Serbian nationalist forces**

**Croatian Control**

**Muslim Control**

**Croatian and Muslim Control**

**Zones protected by the UNPROFOR**

THE ZONES OF CONFLICT IN THE FORMER
YUGOSLAVIA DURING 1992–93

| | |
|---|---|
| c | is pronounced "ts" |
| č | is "ch" |
| ć | is "tu" as in "fu*tu*re" |
| dj | is "j" |
| j | is "y" |
| lj | is "liyuh" |
| š | is "sh" |
| ž | is "zh" |

# The Old Bridge

I DID NOT INTEND to be in Skopje, Macedonia, on America's Inauguration Day, 1993. Short of funds, I had planned to take the morning train to Salonika, Greece—the nearest place to get a cash advance on my American Express card. Checking into my hotel four days earlier, I had been told no one in the capital would take credit cards. "Why?" I asked the clerk. "You're not under the UN embargo." "Macedonia is a small country," he replied. "No one knows how big it will be. Maybe only as big as Skopje!"

Gallows humor reigned throughout the Balkans. In Macedonia it carried a particular significance: the only republic of the former Yugoslavia *not* to go to war, this landlocked state remained in a precarious position. Greece, its neighbor to the south, refusing to recognize the republic unless it changed its name and constitution, blocked its admittance into the United Nations and imposed upon it an unofficial embargo; Serbia, its northern neighbor,

1

viewed Macedonia as southern Serbia, while to its east and west, in the capitals of Bulgaria and Albania, respectively, extremist politicians openly entertained irredentist ideas toward the new country. Macedonia might very well end up the size of Skopje.

The capital, meanwhile, was suffering from a severe weather inversion. It was bitterly cold, snow had piled up on the streets and sidewalks and, rumor had it, state-run industries were taking advantage of the low cloud ceiling to release dangerous pollutants from their smokestacks. Visibility was no more than twenty-five meters. The air had a sickly taste. I longed for the south.

What a change from the balmy weather I had found the week before in Herzeg-Novi, Montenegro, a coastal resort near the Croatian border. On the eve of my departure from that sunlit city, two European Community (EC) military monitors I had befriended invited me out for a drink. They were making evacuation plans, they said, in the event of a NATO air strike against the Bosnian Serbs, whose self-styled Parliament was on the verge of rejecting the Geneva Peace Accord. The last time the monitors had been placed on this state of alert, in early December, they had burned their papers and files only to discover a U.S.-led multinational force was invading Somalia — to the surprise and disappointment of many humanitarians and observers in the Balkan theater.

But perhaps this time the international community would act differently. George Bush might leave his presidency on a decisive note, taking action against the perpetrators of the grisliest crimes against humanity Europe has known since World War II. Or would Bill Clinton enter office with a flourish, marshaling forces to bring the Third Balkan War to a close? The monitors were taking no chances: they had lined up a speedboat, for five hundred deutsche marks, to whisk them across the Adriatic to the Italian resort of Bari.

And what will you do? they asked.

"I'm on my way to Skopje," I shrugged. "I guess I'll keep my fingers crossed."

I boarded the bus the next morning with some misgivings. The sun was shining, the sky was blue and empty, and as we climbed the hills and mountains rising from the coastline, Serbian folk songs crackled on the radio. I scanned the horizon for NATO warplanes: nothing. Hours later, in Podgorica, the capital of Montenegro, where at nightfall I would catch the bus to Macedonia, I walked to the park and watched young families and couples taking advantage of the mild weather. They strolled along the trails, they lounged on the grass. The Soviet-made MIG fighter jets that had patrolled the skies on my last visit to this city were nowhere to be seen. A fine time for an air strike, I thought.

Nothing happened. And soon I was in an unheated bus, gunning its engines through the snowbound mountains of Kosovo. At daybreak, in a freezing hotel room in Skopje, I could not stop shivering. I decided to head for Greece as soon as possible.

Nevertheless, late in the afternoon of January 20, I found myself at the American Center in Skopje, our chargé d'affaires having convinced me to stay for its inauguration party. A crowd of Macedonian politicians, artists, and writers had gathered in the library, where a large television screen showed CNN's broadcast of my country's peaceful transition of government. By chance I stood next to Macedonia's president, Kiro Gligorov, an urbane older gentleman widely viewed as the most reasonable leader in the Balkans, and while we watched Bill Clinton take the oath of office, I wondered what Gligorov was thinking.

In my interview with him the day before he had spelled out his country's plight in measured tones. Gligorov was in an unimaginably difficult position: threatened on every side, he led a fractious government beset by dire economic problems and increasingly vocal opposition from the Albanian minority in the western part of his country. Lacking recognition from the EC, the United Nations, and the United States, Macedonia could not secure loans from the World Bank or the International Monetary Fund

(IMF). And Skopje, all but destroyed by an earthquake in 1963, was cluttered with unfinished construction projects; if not for the inversion, a visitor would have seen a skyline jagged with idle cranes.

The smoky room was silent during the ceremony; only when Maya Angelou stepped up to the podium to read her inaugural poem did the guests begin to speak again. The President and I leaned forward to hear her. Gligorov had more than a passing interest in poetry; proud of his country's strong literary tradition, at the conclusion of my interview with him he had presented me with an anthology of Macedonian poetry. Now he stared at Maya Angelou, perplexed, it seemed. "She's not our best poet," I offered. "It's a political statement." Gligorov smiled broadly.

When the party broke up, I joined several humanitarians from Catholic Relief Services in accepting a dinner invitation from an American diplomat attached to the Conference on Security and Cooperation in Europe (CSCE). After traveling alone for more than two months in the former Yugoslavia, I found it disconcerting to sit in a restaurant at a table full of Americans. The dinner conversation, predictably enough, turned to job opportunities. One humanitarian was thinking about applying to the Foreign Service Institute, another wanted to move to New York City. The diplomat, a beefy, middle-aged man, signaled for the bill. "Anyone in refugee work," he concluded, "will have no trouble getting work for the next twenty or thirty years."

I have been thinking about refugees ever since.

Ours is "the age of the refugee," in George Steiner's phrase, the century in which we have grown accustomed to people being forced from their native lands. War, mass expulsion, famine, environmental degradation, human rights violations, and fear of oppression have sent millions upon millions of men, women, and children into exile. Indeed, a whole literature of exile has emerged in the modern age, a body of work predicated on the notion that many of us will die far from our places of birth — and not by choice. In "Conversation about Dante," an essay exploring, among other matters, the ways in which exile informed the poetics of the Florentine master, the Russian poet Osip Mandelstam — himself an "inner exile" and then a victim of Stalin's concentration camps — suggested that "to speak means to be forever on the road." At no point in history have more people endured exile, whether they speak or remain silent. Anyone, it seems, may wind up on the road.

Refugees, like the poor, have always been with us: in the sixteenth and seventeenth centuries Protestants, Catholics, and Jews were expelled from various European countries, and in the nineteenth century, when political upheaval replaced religious persecution as the chief catalyst of exile, it was Frenchmen, Poles, Germans, and Russians who migrated to the New World. In our time, the dissolution of empires — Ottoman, Romanov, Hohenzollern, and Habsburg — uprooted millions of people who found refuge in successor states or across the ocean. In like manner, the end of colonialism, accompanied by the arbitrary drawing up of borders and preferential treatment of certain ethnic groups, continues to spawn civil wars — and refugees. In fact, war is a constant in the history of refugees, but as Gil Loescher, a brilliant student of the global refugee crisis, points out, "only in the twentieth century has international conflict affected entire populations." Armenians, Anatolian Greeks, European Jews, Cambodians, Bosnians, the Tutsi minority in Rwanda, all have been victims of genocide and massive population transfers. This century — the "American century," as John Lukacs calls it — is marked primarily by migration.

The 1951 Geneva Convention defines a refugee as someone with "a well-founded fear of being persecuted in his country of origin for reasons of race, religion, nationality, membership of a particular social group or political opinion." But with the breakup of the Soviet Union and the changing world order, this definition has become too narrow to account for what is viewed as the flood of refugees spilling out of such places as Vietnam, El Salvador, Nicaragua, Rwanda, Somalia, Haiti, Cuba, and, of course, the former Yugoslavia; drawn up after World War II and designed to encompass the thousands of people fleeing Communism, the term has a different meaning in a world no longer governed by the Cold War's strategic imperatives. That bipolar view of international affairs is gone. As politicians, scholars, and journalists search for a new set of organizing principles for our political order, their task is complicated by the fact that at least 100 million people now live in countries in which they do not hold citizenship.

These include more than twenty million refugees, according to the UN High Commissioner for Refugees (UNHCR), the international agency responsible for protecting them — three times the figure recorded in 1980. In addition, there are some twenty-five million internally displaced people, three million in Bosnia alone. And the numbers will only grow in the coming years, increasing the burden on relief organizations.

No organization feels this burden more than the UNHCR. Established in 1951, the agency was expected to fulfill its mandate in no more than three years. But with an annual budget now of $1.3 billion — 30 percent less than what it needs — the agency has become, as a UNHCR spokesman put it, "one of the growth industries of the 1990s."

It is, however, an industry in crisis. In the last five years UNHCR has mounted an increasing number of emergency operations. The litany of man-made disasters is unbearably long: nearly two million Iraqi Kurds, who in the wake of the Gulf War fled to Iran and the border region between Turkey and Iraq; some four million refugees, displaced people, and other victims of the war in the former Yugoslavia; more than 300,000 Somali refugees; 260,000 refugees from Myanmar; 250,000 refugees from Togo; 1.5 million displaced in Armenia, Azerbaijan, and Tadzhikistan; 780,000 Burundian refugees; 800,000 refugees from Rwanda; and so on. By the end of 1993 the UNHCR was helping twenty-three million people in 143 countries: a picture of world-wide disaster that shows no signs of diminishing.

Nothing better illustrates the nature of the humanitarian crisis than the war in Bosnia, where UNHCR and other aid agencies are condemned by besieged and besieging alike; politicians and commentators around the world decry the relief effort, which in the public mind now stands for an insolvable problem of monumental proportions. More than one-third of UNHCR's budget is earmarked for the former Yugoslavia; millions of people, in all of the republics, depend on relief agencies for food, water, shelter, sanitation, and medical care. The Berlin airlift (1948–49) pales in comparison to the size of the operation in Bosnia, which for three years has employed convoys, airdrops, and an airlift to deliver aid. But because in this theater of war humanitarians are the most visible representatives of the international community, they are often blamed for problems born of indecisive policies at the highest levels. The will of the world being weak regarding Bosnia, the relief effort is a convenient target.

But consider this: according to the rules of war, civilian populations are entitled to relief; attacking or harassing the humanitarians delivering aid is a violation of international law. Yet during the war in Bosnia the UN has never been successful in soliciting from its member nations enough personnel, peacekeepers, supplies, and vehicles to deliver aid to all of the suffering. What is worse, Helsinki Watch reports that "disrespect for the Red Cross emblem and relief personnel has been pervasive throughout Bosnia-Herzegovina." From the first days of the war, Bosnian Serbs have besieged cities and towns, destroyed water pumping stations and electrical towers, shelled hospitals and ambulances, stolen food and medicine — clear violations of the Geneva Convention. Will they be held accountable? Probably not. The international community lacks the will to prosecute these war criminals, since it is also negotiating with them for peace. (And the Croats? The Bosnians? No side is blameless when it comes to using relief operations to further their own ends, though the evidence of these atrocities, as with that of crimes against humanity, particularly genocide and systematic rape, is overwhelmingly against the Bosnian Serbs.)

While relief workers contend with snipers and mortar

fire, hijacked convoys and supplies stolen at gunpoint, diplomats and pundits look for scapegoats — the UN, UNHCR, NATO. But it was the international community's decision early in the fighting to treat all sides as victims that makes it impossible now for many people to distinguish between aggressor and aggrieved, or even to say what went wrong in this war — and why. "The failure to deal adequately with such strife, to do something about mass murder and genocide," writes Leslie Gelb, President of the Council on Foreign Relations, "corrodes the essence of a democratic society. If democratic leaders turn away from genocide or merely pretend to combat it, their citizens will drink in the hypocrisy and sink into cynicism." Surely one expression of that cynicism in the West is the widespread feeling that Bosnia's fate does not concern us. It does.

Twice already in the twentieth century the world has witnessed the consequences of inaction in the face of large-scale refugee crises: recall the plights of European Jews in the 1930s and Palestinians in the 1950s. The terrors of Nazi aggression and the Holocaust should have alerted us to the dangers of isolationism, while the fallout from allowing Palestinian refugees to languish in camps — economic privation, two wars with Israel, a radicalized population, international terrorism, forty years of failed diplomatic initiatives — is immeasurable. Neville Chamberlain is remembered chiefly for believing Hitler's designs on

Czechoslovakia did not concern the British: a fatal error. What Chamberlain called "a quarrel in a faraway country between people of whom we know nothing" was the prelude to World War II and the subsequent deaths of millions.

Perhaps those responsible for the international dithering in the face of Serbian expansionism will be viewed in the same harsh light as this century's most famous architect of appeasement. (Secretary of State Warren Christopher may already have secured such a place in history by describing this war as "a humanitarian crisis a long way from home, in the middle of another continent.") When foreign ministers from Britain, France, Russia, and the United States, meeting in Washington in May 1993, decided to create "safe areas" in Bosnia (which were neither safe nor defensible) in which hundreds of thousands of Muslims could find refuge, Bosnian President Alija Izetbegović responded with a furious indictment of the West: "If the international community is not ready to defend the principles which it itself has proclaimed as its foundations, let it say so openly, both to the people of Bosnia and to the people of the world. Let it proclaim a new code of behavior in which force will be the first and the last argument." Thousands of his own homeless soldiers may well take him at his word. The war in Bosnia and its legacies will be with us for a long time to come.

---

I made five journeys to the former Yugoslavia between August 1992 and September 1994. I arrived in Slovenia just as the first reports appeared in the media of Serbian-run concentration camps in Bosnia, and my last trip to Bosnia coincided with Pope John Paul II's visit to Croatia. My travels, which lasted five months, took me to all of the republics of Yugoslavia — literally, "Land of the South Slavs": a land, as historian Ivo Banac points out, afflicted with "the legend of romantic barbarism and heroic chivalry," at least in the Western imagination. The diplomatic view of this part of the world is decidedly more cynical. At the end of the nineteenth century, Bismarck dismissed problems in this region as "petty local feuds ... not worth the healthy bones of a single Pomeranian grenadier"; yet in this last decade of the twentieth century, the international community is mired, perhaps inextricably, in the Third Balkan War.

Yugoslavia began as an idea among progressive intellectuals in the heady days of the "springtime of nations," an idea destined to fail. The collapse of the Ottoman Empire, which gave rise to two savage Balkan Wars (1912–13), and the destruction of the Habsburg Empire in World War I, universally acknowledged to have begun with the assassination (by a Serbian nationalist) of Archduke Franz Ferdinand on a street in Sarajevo, set the stage, at the Paris Peace Conference, for the creation of the Kingdom of

Serbs, Croats, and Slovenes, the first or royal Yugoslavia. This state became the Kingdom of Yugoslavia in 1929, when Serbian King Alexander assumed dictatorial powers. He was assassinated in 1934, and although he was succeeded by his son Peter II, who operated under the regency of his uncle, Prince Paul, Hitler's invasion in 1941 meant the end of the Kingdom.

The most enduring version of Yugoslavia was forged in Partisan warfare waged against the Axis powers—and against other Yugoslavs. After the civil war, in which 1.2 million Yugoslavs were killed (most of whom "must be reckoned active or passive victims of the policy of Partisan warfare," military historian John Keegan writes), Partisan leader Josip Broz (1891–1980)—or Marshal Tito, as he was known to the world—and his Communist henchmen took control of the government. This "self-managed, non-aligned" Yugoslavia played a middle game between the East and West, acquiring arms from the Soviet Bloc while negotiating loans from the World Bank and the IMF. Tito ruled the country with an iron fist, balancing the needs of the republics and suppressing expressions of nationalism. Not surprisingly, when he died it was nationalists who rose to power in each republic, particularly in Serbia, where Slobodan Milošević called for "a Greater Serbia," a dream of ethnic purity at odds with demographics and borders. "Born in violence," Mark Thompson writes of Yugoslavia, "it could only be maintained by force." That force was what eventually tore it apart.

The third incarnation of Yugoslavia vanished in June 1991, when Slovenia and Croatia, the northern (and richest) republics, which had long complained about Serbian centralization in federal affairs, seceded from the country. The Yugoslav National Army (JNA), one of the largest standing forces in Europe, waged a half-hearted attempt to secure Slovenia's borders only to be rebuffed by that republic's well-armed militia. Milošević and his generals, some commentators have argued, were prepared to let go of Slovenia, an ethnically homogenous society. They had different designs on Croatia, which had a large Serbian population and a murderous past in the infamous Ustaša regime of World War II. (Led by Ante Pavelić, a fanatical Croatian nationalist with the support of Italian Fascists, the Ustaše tried to annihilate the Serbs. Theirs was a simple formula: "Kill a third, convert a third [of the Serbian Orthodox Christians to Catholicism], expel a third." Three hundred and fifty thousand to 450,000 Serbs, Jews, and Gypsies were executed, almost half of them at one concentration camp, Jasenovac.) In Tito's Yugoslavia, the Serbs did not forget the war crimes of the Ustaše, whose barbaric methods even German Nazis deemed excessive. Thus when Slovenia's relatively bloodless Ten-Day — or Television — War ended in early July, the JNA attacked Croatia, ushering in the most savage fighting on the Continent since World War II, the Serbian-dominated army capturing one-third of the republic, including the area around Jasenovac.

It was then the refugee crisis in the Balkans began. "Ethnic cleansing," a brutal program of forced population transfers and genocide, entered the lexicon of the age: thousands of people lost their lives, thousands more fled burning villages and cities. A cease-fire worked out by UN Special Envoy Cyrus Vance in January 1992 offered only temporary respite. Yugoslavia's most ethnically diverse republic, Bosnia-Herzegovina (44% Muslim, 31% Serb, 17% Croat), was Milošević's next target. In March 1992 the republic passed a referendum on independence, which was boycotted by the Bosnian Serbs. In April, when the EC recognized Bosnia-Herzegovina (hereafter referred to as Bosnia), the JNA teamed up with the Bosnian Serbs to attack the new state. The horror visited upon Croatia was magnified in Bosnia. The UN-imposed arms embargo on Yugoslavia, which favored the heavily-armed JNA (and the Bosnian Serbs who inherited the army's weapons when Milošević made a show of removing his troops), enabled the Serbs to consolidate their gains, and soon they occupied 70 percent of Bosnia. Millions of people were displaced from their homes; not since the immediate aftermath of World War II have there been so many refugees in Europe.

Once fighting broke out in Bosnia, UNHCR found itself in a peculiar position. Having opened offices in Bosnia to take care of refugees from Croatia, the agency for the first time had to set up a relief operation "in country." UNHCR took the lead, supplemented by three UN humanitarian agencies, the World Health Organisation (WHO), the World Food Programme (WFP), and UNICEF, as well as by many nongovernmental organizations (NGOs), including the International Rescue Committee (IRC), *Mèdecins Sans Frontières* (MSF), the Lutheran World Federation, and Oxfam. Furthermore, the charity of private citizens like George Soros, the international financier who contributed millions of dollars, was indispensable. Twenty-four thousand members of the UN Protection Forces (UNPROFOR), the troops responsible for maintaining peace and security and providing for the safe delivery of humanitarian aid, were scattered around Bosnia; these peacekeepers, the majority of whom came from France and Britain, suffered more than five hundred casualties in three years.

Most of the internationals in Bosnia, then, are peacekeepers, humanitarians, or journalists. What impressed me during my travels there was the heroism of ordinary men and women working for relief agencies. It is right to denounce the ways in which humanitarian operations were used to justify Western inaction: the safety of the peacekeepers and relief workers was a shield behind which Bosnian Serbs waged war with impunity. (French and British politicians were particularly adept at discouraging military intervention, promoting humanitarian efforts and diplomatic solutions long after it became clear that Radovan Karadžić, leader of the Bosnian Serbs, had no interest in a negotiated peace — a policy which led Sarajevans to say they were being fattened up for slaughter.) And only a fool would turn a blind eye to the corruption, endemic in war, goods being in short supply, at every level of the UN; that UNHCR and UNPROFOR are in urgent need of reform is common knowledge in relief circles. Still, I marveled at the courage of those who would choose to live among the aggrieved, especially the humanitarians, who unlike UNPROFOR are not equipped to defend themselves.

Certainly humanitarians are no less fallible than the rest of humankind, except insofar as they regularly risk their lives to help people in distant places. I met plenty of backbiters and incompetents who worked for relief agencies, as well as those who were lazy and venal, but what I remember with deep admiration is the humanitarian community's courageous efforts — the work of thousands of people — to shore back up a crumbling world. Robert Frost called poetry "a momentary stay against confusion"; a relief operation is a stay against death and despair.

Journalists record the tragedy, humanitarians salve the pain of the suffering. Only a writer with a hard heart would not envy the humanitarian's efforts — and occasional successes.

But it is failure in Bosnia we will remember — the failure of the international community to intervene and put an end to the suffering. Future historians, policy makers, and diplomats will learn to recite the signs of that failure: round after round of futile negotiations with the so-called warring factions, the deepening realization that once again appeasement of an aggressor did not work, the fracturing of the Western alliance, NATO's loss of credibility. And the measure of our failure? More than 200,000 dead or missing, nearly a million wounded, millions of refugees. "Exile begets exile," writes Edward Said, a Palestinian exile who knows full well the dangers of dispossession. We have not even begun to know the consequences of our collective failure in Bosnia.

Harris Burina, the comic actor from Sarajevo, was the proverbial man without a country. He had made his reputation in the capital, performing in more than a dozen films, earning awards, acclaim, and enough money, he said, to live in style. But the crowning moment of his career in Yugoslavia — he and ten other Bosnian actors had spent the year before the war working in Belgrade, where his last role had been in a Serbo-Croatian production of Lanford Wilson's *Burn This*—had cost him his future in Bosnia. He believed his countrymen would always view him with suspicion.

I met Harris and his wife in Ljubljana, Slovenia, in August 1992, when they were waiting for French visas; with luck they would soon fly to Paris, where he hoped to rejoin his Bosnian theater troupe, which had gone into exile. The Burinas had no time to lose: they had only a thousand deutsche marks and one-week Slovene visas.

"I played the golden years in Sarajevo," he said one afternoon in Drama, a popular bar, "and now it is finished."

He was suffering from a severe hangover—he and his wife had drunk seven bottles of wine since lunch the day before—so he was alternating glasses of water with mugs of beer, chain-smoking at the bar. He was a slim man with black hair, thick black eyebrows, and an earring; his colorful shirt was the brightest object in the dimly lit room. His wife, a striking woman with shoulder-length blond hair, was talking with a Slovene screenwriter named Stojan who had gone to meet them at the airport. Stojan was their guide in Ljubljana, and it pained him that he could help Harris but not his own cousin, who was still trapped in Sarajevo.

A heavy rain was falling outside. Harris ordered another round of drinks.

"For that year in Belgrade I was a superstar," he said. "My job was just theater, film, giving interviews. The best ever. Now they're killing us. Serb terrorists came to my home in Belgrade and told me to leave the country. It was a *theater* director," he shouted, "who waved his gun at me. He belonged to the White Eagles, the worst fanatics.

"I can't work for my people either because I played in Belgrade. So I'm living every day in pictures, in my memories, since my parents and friends are still there."

Despite his hangover and visible despair, he had not lost his sense of irony. Fleeing to Macedonia, he had made it across the border only because the guard, recognizing him from his films, had looked the other way. (Much the same thing had happened at Brnk Airport in Ljubljana, according to Stojan. "Let Burina through," the border guard was told over the phone.) In Skopje, Harris took a job as a bartender in a pub, where the patrons kept looking for cameras. This must be a movie set! they thought.

That story reminded Harris of a friend who went to America with twenty thousand worthless Yugoslav bank-notes, each bearing a picture of Nikola Tesla, the Croatian-born electrician whose inventions included systems of arc lighting and wireless communication. Tesla had emigrated to the United States in 1884, and in America he is remembered best for constructing the first power station at Niagara Falls—a fact Harris's friend turned to his advantage. He set up a stand by Tesla's monument in the state park at Niagara Falls and sold his suitcase full of 500-dinar notes to honeymooning couples for five dollars apiece. In three days he made $80,000. His only regret was that he had not brought a million dinars.

Harris told these stories with glee, gesturing wildly, now smoothing back his hair, now lighting another cigarette. Then his mood changed. "Maybe I can never return to Bosnia," he sighed. "I was everywhere, and now it's finished. People in New York and Paris and London gave me chances before, but I always said I must stay in my country. For ten years I was one of Bosnia's best cultural ambassadors to the world. 'I'm a Sarajevo actor,' I used to say. Now I just want to leave. Belgrade, Skopje, Ljubljana . . . they're no longer mine. And I played for Yugoslavia.

"Everything comes in phases. Now I'm in the second half of my life. What was before is over. I lived for five years in a hotel in Sarajevo, every day as if it were my last. I never knew if I would wake up in the morning. I was rich, and I didn't buy a house. I know ten millionaires with big houses, and they left with shopping bags. Now we're the same. I'm twenty-nine years old. I'm lucky I played half my life as an actor. Maybe it's all over. Or maybe I'll be good in Paris. Anything is possible. I have to learn French, then English. I'm living so fast." He took a drink. "In Belgrade they said I'm better than John Malkovich. It's true. I have sparks, hair, and energy, like the space shuttle!"

Perhaps only in the Balkans could a comparison be made between this comic actor and the demonic star of *Dangerous Liaisons* and *Empire of the Sun*. Likewise, it was hard to believe that Sarajevans, who prided themselves on their cosmopolitanism, would reject their native son because he had worked in Belgrade. But I said nothing, unlike his wife, who kept interrupting him to ask questions. His replies grew more and more abrupt. All he had left, he told me, were his memories and his wife.

"If you don't watch your step," I said, "you may end up with only memories."

Harris stared off into the distance. He took a sip of water, drained his beer, and ordered more drinks. "What can I do? I must help my parents," he said suddenly. "They have no food. You can't imagine. I called my father and said, 'I'm so upset now that I can't see you.' He said, 'Don't be upset. This is my second war. Everything is destiny.' And me? What I did in Sarajevo is history."

He lit another cigarette. "Do you know there are so many refugees in Ljubljana that every night at the disco is Sarajevo night? And here you have the same divisions between people that you have in Bosnia."

"So many voices, so many shootings," said Emir Grcič, recalling the Serbian invasion of Brčko, a Bosnian town eighty miles northeast of Sarajevo. It was on 5 May 1992 that Grcič, a former first-division soccer player in Yugoslavia and Turkey, began a terrifying odyssey that ended a year later in the summer of 1993, when he arrived at his new home in Seattle, where I spent a day with him and his family. "God save me, I was thinking. I am not guilty for anything," he said in heavily inflected English. "Or kill me normal, not like a dog."

One month after the war began, Grcič and sixteen other Muslims from his apartment building were rounded up by Serbian militiamen under the leadership of a man who called himself Hitler. "I've killed 75 people," said this commander, waving his gun. "I will kill you all."

He singled out Grcič. "You have blue eyes. You are Ustaša," he told the Muslim athlete. "You are a sniper, like me."

"I don't know how to shoot," Grcič pleaded. "I am a sportsman, not a soldier."

His protest fell on deaf ears. He prepared himself for death. Two by two his neighbors — all men, all civilians — were led out into the street and executed. Six had already died when Grcič was taken from the building to be shot. He was grateful that his wife, Enisa, had fled with their two young sons to Split, Croatia; his argument that the fighting in Vukovar, Dubrovnik, and now Sarajevo would not spill over into Brčko had proved wrong.

"I think, okay, no problem, I lived," he remembered. "Then a car stopped, and a Serb called my name. He knew me as a soccer player. He said, 'Save this man. He's honest. He's a sportsman.'"

And they let him go.

For two months, hiding first in his apartment (until the Serbs patrolling the streets looted and destroyed it), then with his sister-in-law (who was married to a Serb), Grcič could only wonder what would happen next. The personal crisis he had faced before the war was far from his mind. Twelve years of professional soccer had taken its toll on his body. It was time to consider a new career — coaching, perhaps, or refereeing. He had played for clubs at all levels in Serbia, Croatia, Bosnia, Slovenia, and Istanbul, with players of every ethnic background in the former Yugoslavia; he had made several appearances with the Bosnian National Team, earning a reputation as a skilled, honest player. Though he had studied law at the University of Sarajevo, Grcič knew instinctively that soccer was his life. What he did not know was that his next chance to play would be in a concentration camp, in boots, on a snow-covered street.

Arrested again, he spent the next eight months in Batkovič, where as many as one hundred men were murdered by the Serbs. "Every five days they would shoot somebody to frighten us," he told me. And if a Serbian soldier lost his life in, say, Brčko, a prisoner from the same town would be executed in retaliation. Grcič was forced to dig trenches near the front lines, where his own countrymen fired at him, and to cut wood in groves frequently struck by artillery. Many prisoners, especially old men and children, could not survive on their diet of bread and thin soup, no salt or sugar. Grcič himself lost more than 50 pounds. The soccer match? It was played for the benefit of UNHCR officials visiting the camp. His captors, Grcič believed, would do anything to avoid war crimes charges.

Upon his release in a prisoner exchange in March 1993, Grcič was put to work digging trenches for the Bosnian army—a task he was removed from after two days because he was too weak to lift a shovel. Then, escaping across the country, first in an ambulance driven by a friend, then on foot and by taxi, he made his way to the Croatian border, leaving his parents and younger brother behind. At last he came to Split, where he saw his wife for the first time in a year. His sons, Amar and Adi, aged eight and five, respectively, did not recognize him.

And still he did not feel safe. The rising tension between Croats and Muslims, which would soon erupt into brutal fighting in central Bosnia, as well as his experiences in Brčko and Batkovič, convinced him that his family could no longer live among people "schooled for killing."

"I cannot explain such hate," he told me. "These are not

human beings. They are animals. They are drugged. They are a motive without reason."

It was only by chance that in Split Grcič heard about a U.S. government's refugee resettlement program for those who had been in concentration camps. With help from IRC, he applied to the program. He was the last one in his group to qualify, causing him to think for a second time his life had been miraculously spared.

Like their fellow refugees, the Grcičs did not know where they would be sent in the United States until just before they left Croatia. Their host family and representatives of an aid agency met them at the Seattle airport, and within days they had an apartment, money, and green cards. Grcič immediately started looking for work, though he had the drawn look of someone who had returned from the dead. His blond hair was cropped, his features seemed too angular, and although he had regained most of the weight lost in Batkovič, he understood that no one can survive such an ordeal and not be marked. But he had a ready smile, a quick laugh. He wore the same red soccer sweater he had worn the day of his first arrest and near-execution, and then throughout his stay in camp, but Grcič was determined to put his recent past behind him.

"I want to find good things to remember and move on. I lost two houses and my car but I am lucky. A lot of people lost everything, and now they are dead."

In the Refugee Resettlement office in Seattle he watched his sons kick a plastic inflatable globe that was bigger than a beach ball. Their laughter filled the air. He wanted to teach them to be sportsmen, as his father had taught him. He told me Adi, the youngest, had the heart of a soccer player. In fact, the boy ran recklessly about the room, and when he fell, he shrieked with delight. Enisa was afraid that soon she might wake from a dream and discover their good fortune had changed. She would start English lessons within the week.

And his own plans?

"I want to play again," he said wistfully. "I just want a chance here. I know I'm not in real form yet. I need one or two months to get in shape. But I have a lot of experience, and now I don't have to run as much."

Harris Burina and his wife were blessed with youth (which in humanitarian circles translates into *adaptability,* the willingness to start new lives), talent, connections, and enough money to travel abroad. Emir Grcič had a remarkable streak of good luck. But most refugees are ordinary people possessing ordinary kinds of luck. In August 1994, three years after the JNA had begun to wage war against Slovenia and Croatia, millions of refugees and displaced persons remained in the former Yugoslavia.

In Croatia, some 380,000 people (approximately 10

percent of the total population) were registered with UNHCR; divided about evenly between those displaced by the fighting in Croatia and in Bosnia, this figure was roughly half of what it had been at its peak less than a year earlier. (Some had returned to Dubrovnik and parts of Croatian-held territory in Slavonia, others had gone to third countries, and still others, having assimilated into their new surroundings, no longer bothered to apply for aid.) Housed in hotels and schools, in military barracks and private homes, the refugees in their various makeshift arrangements were a prominent feature of every locale in this war-torn country.

One day I visited two camps on the outskirts of Zagreb. My translator, Marina Pintarić, was a student at the university. She had postponed her exams the previous year in order to translate for a Spanish humanitarian organization; like many bright young people in the Balkans, she took advantage of her skills to earn much more money working for an international aid agency than she could hope to make otherwise. But this day she was reluctant to go to the first camp, a rehabilitation center located next to a hospital that had once served the JNA, because she used to go there to visit a boy afflicted with cerebral palsy.

"I don't like to be seen here now," she said at the door.

Many of these refugees were from Vukovar, the Croatian city that in the first months of fighting had endured some of the most intense bombardment in the history of modern warfare: more shells landed per square meter there than during the siege of Stalingrad. When the city fell in November 1991 the JNA took 300 patients from the hospital and massacred them. Croatian television was now reporting twelve hundred people were still missing from the area. Marina realistically expected to be greeted with bitterness at the rehabilitation center — only the year before, interviewing other refugees from Vukovar, I had been overcome by their anger and despair — but these older men and women had apparently reconciled themselves to their fates.

Indeed, the first refugee we met was so cheerful that I grew suspicious of her optimism. Živka Garbac was a laughing, white-haired woman, dressed in a black skirt and a blue muscle T-shirt emblazoned with two palm trees and an English inscription: SUNDAY. She described her garden and the produce she shared with other refugees, her work in the kitchen, the cakes she baked for the children in the center. Only the day before she had prepared a pig for her grandson's wedding. He had been wounded in the head and stomach, then imprisoned. Upon his release, Croatian authorities gave him a house on the Adriatic that had probably once belonged to a Serbian family. Now he was about to marry. Živka's husband and son had not survived the siege. She had also lost both of her houses and everything she owned except the clothes she was wearing. This she told me with a smile.

She introduced me to her "boyfriend," a retired coal miner named Nikola Rakarić. He said his entire family had fought in the war: men, women, children, grandchildren, and a great-grandchild. He came from a village near Topusko, famous for its hot springs and spa. "When I retired, I spent my time farming," he said. "I had two horses, cows, pigs. I had my own forest and meadow. But I could see this coming. We had no weapons, and the Serbs were fully armed. They were bringing in guns for a long time, on helicopters and airplanes."

He showed me a photograph of his grandson in uniform. His son, he said proudly, had been on the front lines since the beginning of the war. "They burned my house and took all my animals. In my village they burned the church last. The only thing they can't take is the land." He stared out the window. "You could boil an egg in that hot spring," he said sadly. "In Austro-Hungarian times the soldiers used to heal themselves there. They were going to expand the spa, but the war stopped that. Now it's only water."

Through the afternoon we listened to stories of destroyed houses and churches, ruined orchards and vineyards. One old Bosnian couple and their neighbors had hid in their basement while the Serbs burned their house down. All had lost loved ones. And all wanted to return to their villages and towns (now under Serbian control), even if it meant living in a tent, as one refugee said. Only the last woman who talked to us, eighty-three-year-old Katarina Gašparović, did not want to go back. She had thick arms and a heavily lined face, her red hair balding at the top. She came from Rakovica, near Plitvica, once the most popular national park in Yugoslavia; before the war, 10,000 people a day had visited the region southwest of Zagreb, hiking to its lakes and through its deep forests, where bears, wolves, and wild boars lived. Katarina had been in the refugee center for almost three years.

"Our village was attacked for months," she said, "but we kept working, going into the basements during the bombing. On November 15, eight tanks entered the village. People started to flee. I didn't want to leave my son, who was in the army. But he had a bad leg and couldn't go anywhere. And he trusted the Serbs. He was an electrician before the war, he wired all their houses. When he stayed behind, I went with a man on a tractor into the forest."

But gunfire raked the woods, and then their tractor ran out of gas. After three days and nights, a friend came and took them to another village, where they stayed through five weeks of fighting. At last she and other refugees boarded buses for Bosnia that went only a few kilometers before being stopped by artillery fire.

"We had to walk forty kilometers through the woods,

from four in the afternoon until sunrise. We came to a village in Bosnia where we had tea, and more buses came to take us to Zagreb."

*"Forty kilometers,"* said Marina, shaking her head.

"Yes, I had a stroke," said the old woman. "I was five weeks in a hospital and five more in a spa. I knit when I can but my hand is bad, it is often blocked. I'm the only one here from that part of Croatia, because I'm the only one with family in Zagreb. My daughter works with the invalids. My son? They killed him. And then they burned my village down."

Tears welled in her eyes. "In World War II, the Serbs killed my husband. Now they have killed my son. I stayed alone with four children after the last war. My oldest daughter died seven years ago. And now they have killed my youngest son."

On our way out of the center we met Živka again. She showed us photographs of her son's wedding and funeral. "I was in an asylum during his funeral," she said. She gave me a gift, a handstitched doily. "I lost two brothers in World War II," she continued. "I lost a grandson in a car accident. I lost my husband and son in this war. I have some kind of curse on my family." And then she left.

Outside, Marina said, "When I was translating for the Spanish, we heard these stories all the time. 'I lost my father, my brother, my husband, my son,' they'd say. Then I'd have to ask, 'What are your needs? Five kilos of sugar?' It's crazy. What they need is what no one can give them — a father, a brother, a husband, a son."

We went on to another refugee camp, where more than a hundred Croats from central Bosnia were crammed into a converted barracks and ten huts fashioned out of sheet metal. In one hut the size of a small guest bedroom lived a family of nine. "My father," a little boy said proudly, pointing at the hut, "is an epileptic."

Relief workers from France *Libertés* had spent the previous four days setting up an outdoor miniature circus. Actors taught the children to juggle; a film crew recorded the rehearsals; the next night there would be a performance, and then the humanitarians would pack up their masks, costumes, ring, curtains, and go home.

Raifa, a large woman who was in charge of the camp, led us into the barracks and assembled eight women in a space no bigger than a college dormitory room. A clothesline stretched from the only window to the door, and curtains hid her family's belongings. While the women, ranging in age from thirty to seventy, sat on a pair of beds and knitted, Raifa made strong Turkish coffee for Marina and me. In her village of Gračanica, she said, she had owned a three-story house with nine large rooms.

"If somebody had told me someday I would live, cook, and wash dishes in one room, I would have killed myself," she laughed.

Their living conditions were abysmal. One washing machine, one ten-liter hot water heater, two filthy tubs for bathing. Families of six or seven people slept in a single room. The unlighted hallway was lined with shoes, potatoes, onions, lockers, cardboard boxes, and split wood. Three toilets served the entire camp.

"We came in May 1992," said Ruža, a handsome woman dressed in red. "Only older women and children could go. The rest had to stay and fight. Our army fought the Serbs for three months and lost. Serbs occupy our village. We don't know what became of our houses. We came to Zagreb because before the war our husbands worked in a factory here. The factory turned this place into a camp."

What do you miss most? I asked the women.

"Everything," Iva, the youngest, giggled, "and the fact that our families are split up. My sister's in Germany, my brother's on the front. And that's typical."

Raifa took us on a brief tour of the camp. We began with the bathroom, where I was nearly overcome by the stench, and ended near the circus, where children wearing masks and costumes were playing. The air was alive with laughter. The French humanitarians eyed us suspiciously. Raifa's oldest son, dressed as a clown, asked me for sweets. She twisted his ear, smiling.

"The children go to school," she said, patting him on the head. "They have no problems with their classmates, but they have no books. And us? We get up in the morning, we take coffee, we talk, we knit. Winter is coming, so we have to make new socks."

"Do you have any hope of returning?" I said.

"Those who come from occupied villages have their doubts." She sighed. "We go to church every Sunday to meet the other Bosnians. Only God knows how long this will last. We never thought we would be here this long."

The sky was overcast when Marina and I left the camp. Rain was on its way. I recalled what Marina's older sister, Jadranka, had said about refugees in Croatia: "They're like people who have lost a limb. Amputees. They can still feel their homeland, even though it's gone. It tingles. Subconsciously they know everything was destroyed, but as long as they're in a camp they can dream it's still there. Those who integrate into society know they'll never go back, those in camps all believe they'll return."

Marina led me through a vacant lot and soon we came to a wide thoroughfare. We walked past Croatia's only film studio; on this day it was deserted. In the parking lot were four rusted trucks and some abandoned props. Marina let out a long sigh.

"Frightening," she said. "Three years they've been in that camp, and you see how they don't do anything to fix it up? They could paint those rooms. They could pool their resources and buy some paint. Or ask the factory for money. And the smell in Raifa's room! It always smells like that. It comes from cooking with too much grease in a small place."

Marina's anger was born of frustration. Rebel Serbs in Krajina held 30 percent of Croatia's territory, the tourist industry had collapsed in the wake of the fighting, hotels on the Dalmatian coast were filled with refugees. There were 14,000 UN peacekeepers in Croatia and the economy was in shambles: the war hindered the transition to a market economy (the government was in no hurry to privatize), the refugees strained the country's ability to provide services to its own citizens. And many Croats believed that nothing would change for years to come. In such conditions it was easy to blame the refugees for Croatia's problems.

"Frightening," Marina repeated.

How to stem the tide of war refugees? Solve the problem at its source, before it becomes unmanageable — that is, resolve conflicts before the shooting starts. It is very much harder to stop a war than to prevent one. Barring superpower rivalries, our future conflicts will likely be what Leslie Gelb calls "teacup wars," seemingly endless skirmishes around the world, which will produce more refugees and civilian casualties than the democratic West can tolerate. Preventative diplomacy, like preventative medicine, must be the watchword for the next century.

After all, "aid fatigue" (the term used to describe the reluctance of developed nations to continue donating to people caught up in what look like inextricable problems) set in long ago.

Imagine, for example, if Secretary of State James Baker had acted with discernment during his infamous trip to Belgrade in June 1991, insisting that Slobodan Milošević sit down with leaders from the other Yugoslav republics and negotiate a peaceful transition to a confederation. By most accounts Baker told the Serbian president the U.S. government valued, above all, Yugoslavia's integrity — that is, he gave Milošević permission to keep the country together at any cost. A tragic mistake — and avoidable: the CIA had warned the Bush administration that civil war was in the offing. Baker played down their counsel. And he was responsible for the disastrous decision to impose an arms embargo on Yugoslavia, which left the Croats and Bosnians almost defenseless against the well-armed JNA.

And once the fighting began, what then? The United States and its allies *had* the military and economic power to make the belligerents negotiate in good faith. Early on, George Bush deferred to the Europeans, who mistakenly believed they could work in a concerted fashion to bring the combatants to their senses. And when the EC was unable to present a united front on security issues (thanks in part to Germany's hasty recognition of Slovenia and Croatia in December 1991), Bush ducked the chance to take the lead, despite the triumphant example of a half-century of American leadership in Europe, his own success in Desert Storm, and mounting pressure to end the bloodshed.

Bill Clinton only complicated matters. Notwithstanding his campaign promises to lift the arms embargo on the Bosnians and to use NATO air strikes to stop Serbian aggression, President Clinton squandered the considerable power of his office, now proposing to act, now giving in to the wishes of diplomats in London and Paris. His uncertainty had international repercussions: by the summer of 1993, James Chace, editor of *World Policy Journal,* could announce the collapse of the Western alliance as a result of Clinton's indecision regarding what to do in Bosnia. "If ever there were a time for visionary statesmanship," Chace wrote, lamenting the absence of figures like George Kennan and George Marshall, Konrad Adenauer and Jean Monnet, the inspired architects of the post–World War II international order, "that time is now." Sadly, Clinton was not up to the task. Nor were his European counterparts.

In fact, a credible threat of force is the only language most tyrants understand, and NATO possessed such credibility, at least until the Bihać debacle in November 1994, when it became obvious the West would not intervene to protect the UN-mandated "safe area." Long before this final insult, however, the policy of appeasing the aggressors had shown itself to be bankrupt. "The Serbs concluded that nobody would come to the rescue of Bosnia," Fouad Ajami writes in his elegy for Sarajevo:

> An old legend about the martial virtues of the Serbs (a legend like the one that was circulating about Iraq's Republican Guard before that particular bluff was called) served as an excuse for Western abdication. It was the passivity of the United States in the period of its global primacy that put the Bosnians and their cause in great peril. And so it was that the city that lived on sufferance became the city that lived on suffering.

"The American abdication," this scholar adds, "never even paid the Bosnians the compliment of candor. The truth of our inaction had to be covered up; and so our cavalry was always a day or a provocation away." The lesson, of course, was not lost on tyrants in Somalia, Rwanda, North Korea, Haiti, and elsewhere. When the U.S. had the chance to act responsibly, it flinched, and the barbarians — Constantine Cavafy called an earlier incarnation of these despots "a kind of solution" — won the day. They are the ones establishing the governing principles for the new world order.

———————

*Maybe Airlines* was what peacekeepers called the UNHCR airlift, which in addition to delivering humanitarian supplies ferried internationals into and out of the besieged capital. On one of my trips to Sarajevo, in October 1993, I was met at the airport by a fellow alumnus from high school. What a strange place to see Kent Morris for the first time in twenty years! A sturdy, dark-haired man with a mustache and a sardonic wit, he was working for IRC, and as he drove me in an Armored Personnel Carrier (APC) toward the city, he caught me up on his life. He had been the only one in his graduating class *not* to go directly to college, enlisting instead in the Navy, a radical notion in 1974: the year before Saigon fell, students from our prep school in New Jersey were not passing up college for the military. But Kent's stints abroad and his training in special operations would prove useful in his next career — disaster relief. After earning undergraduate and graduate degrees at Columbia, in international affairs and Middle East studies, Kent served in Desert Storm as a political and cultural affairs specialist. His next assignment, in the Balkans, offered a dramatic illustration of the lesson that in the new world order the principles of war may be applied to relief operations.

His first stop was Mostar, the city in western Herzegovina that had withstood some of the most savage fighting of the war, first in attacks from the Bosnian Serbs (backed up by the JNA), then in battles between Croats and Muslims. The writer Misha Glenny awarded Miodrag Perušić, the mad JNA commander who in the first month of fighting began the systematic destruction of Herzegovina's capital, "first prize in the keenly contested 'Most Bloodthirsty General' stakes of the Yugoslav wars." The JNA relentlessly bombarded Mostar's beautiful Ottoman architecture, including the famous old footbridge arcing high above the Neretva River; the civilian population, Muslim and Croat, was cruelly starved.

That was not the end of it. Though Mostar's Serbs, Croats, and Muslims had distinguished themselves in World War II by resisting what Glenny calls "the temptation of mutual loathing which gripped the rest of western and eastern Herzegovina and the Neretva valley," in the Third Balkan War they succumbed to their worst impulses. After the Serbian onslaught, in April 1993 the Bosnian Croatian Army (HVO) in West Mostar turned against their erstwhile allies and trained their guns on the Muslims across the river. Like the Serbs, the HVO set up concentration camps, summarily executed Muslims, and blocked UN humanitarian convoys. By August 1993 Croat authorities had denied aid to East Mostar for two months, and 55,000 Muslims were starving. Only a series of BBC reports on the "deplorable" conditions in the besieged part of the city, which galvanized international opinion, forced the UN to act.

Officials from UNPROFOR Civil Affairs negotiated an agreement with the HVO permitting a humanitarian convoy to travel to East Mostar. What followed was a perfect example of a relief operation gone awry. The problems began even before the convoy left the Herzeg — or Croatian — Bosnian town of Medjugorje, where UNHCR, the International Committee of the Red Cross (ICRC), and NGOs had their offices. (A telltale irony: in 1981 a vision of the Virgin Mary was supposedly vouchsafed to six children in Medjugorje, and when the town became a religious mecca the government, anticipating a tourist boom, built several hotels that, during the war, were often occupied by relief workers and refugees.) The Bosnian Croats refused to let the convoy leave unless a special delivery of humanitarian aid was also made to West Mostar. The UN agreed to this demand, but Croatian authorities did not allow the additional trucks sent from Metković, Croatia, to cross the border into Herzeg-Bosnia, and so the convoy was postponed until the next morning.

By noon all the trucks were in Medjugorje and ready to make the short journey to Mostar. On the outskirts of town, however, a crowd of demonstrators blocked the convoy. After an hour and a half of negotiations, an old woman dressed in black was hoisted atop one truck, where she determined that the Muslims would receive only bags of flour, not munitions — a performance staged for the

Croatian media and foreign press. She gave the convoy her blessing, but the trucks drove only twelve kilometers before being stopped, twice in 300 meters, by crowds of angry refugees from central Bosnia, who demanded food and housing—from the Croatian government.

The demonstrators were not cleared away until early evening, and when the convoy resumed more refugees and local residents lined the road, hurling curses and stones. At dusk the trucks started slowly down the mountain road into Mostar. Kent saw grass fires and burning houses on the nearby hills. By the airport, the "no-man's land" where the trucks would be divided and sent to a makeshift hospital or to one of two warehouses, anti-aircraft airbursts lit up the sky. UN military observers drove ahead to exchange the remains of HVO and Bosnian soldiers, and confirm the cease-fire. No one seemed to know how to find the hospital or warehouses—the maps were useless—and as soon as the convoy entered Bosnian territory a truck drove into a ditch. It was after midnight when the convoy arrived in East Mostar.

Military transport planes were carrying out an airdrop over the city; even with the cease-fire, small arms, rocket-propelled grenades, and mortars fired through the night; a sniper "worked" the intersection the trucks had to cross to reach the hospital. Chaos reigned: Spanish peacekeepers assigned to the area stayed in their APCs when the trucks were unloaded, relief workers gradually abandoned their posts, and while those in charge were distracted, the convoy was blocked by two trucks, a bus, and land mines laid around them. At daybreak, a crowd of Muslims gathered, bearing signs, in English and Serbo-Croatian, denouncing the world for allowing East Mostar to be destroyed.

The blockade was orchestrated by the Bosnian government, which wanted the cease-fire extended, new bridges built across the river, international attention focused on East Mostar's predicament. The Muslims believed that if the UN abandoned them they would die; HVO radio and loudspeaker units were warning the Muslims that once the trucks left they would be massacred. "They had no choice but to fight," said Kent. Meantime, the peacekeepers remained in their APCs—one officer said they needed permission from Madrid just to load their weapons. The convoy personnel wandered away from the trucks. And thousands of local residents, taking advantage of the cease-fire, strolled around East Mostar, though HVO mortars and tanks continued to fire at Bosnian army positions in the city.

At nine in the morning Cedric Thornberry, head of UNPROFOR Civil Affairs, made what my friend called "a leisurely and late tour" of the humanitarian operation. Negotiations proceeded throughout the day to end the blockade and release a Croatian UNHCR driver taken away by Bosnian police. Rumors circulated among the convoy, spread by Thornberry's own subordinates ("They were trying to make names for themselves at his expense," said Kent) as well as by one Sally Becker, an independent humanitarian and HVO apologist who in the early evening appeared in East Mostar. "She walked through the convoy explaining to everyone how she had the power to get the trucks released," he said.

But the HVO was not to blame for the blockade, which was even more upsetting to the Croats than to the UN. Convinced the Bosnian Army was using the temporary peace to move troops and supplies, the HVO threatened to end the cease-fire.

"[The HVO] placed heavy mortar rounds closer to the convoy to show their sincerity," said Kent, who saw Bosnian troops redeploying in the dark, using the convoy as cover.

The relief workers spent the night in the trucks, shortwave BBC broadcasts providing them with more reliable information about the blockade than what the UN was passing along. They had no food or water, and in the morning the peacekeepers agreed to share their rations only when the Bosnian Civil Defense distributed bread and cocoa to the convoy. There was still no word about the negotiations; HVO artillery, mortar, and tank fire crept closer to the convoy. That afternoon the humanitarians were told to prepare to "break out," and though the peacekeepers could have forced the blockade, nothing happened. So they spent another night in Mostar.

They had a rough awakening. At sunrise two HVO heavy artillery rounds landed by their soft-skinned vehicles. They sought shelter in the peacekeepers' APCs, but the Spaniards closed the hatches, despite promises from the commanding officer, a colonel, that the humanitarians would be let in. Not once that morning did the soldiers leave their APCs to provide security. The colonel admitted that his troops "could not be relied on to protect the humanitarians." In other words, they would not fulfill their UNPROFOR mandate. Fortunately, no relief workers were wounded, and later in the afternoon the convoy was finally allowed to return to Medjugorje.

"The whole operation was poorly planned for [execution in] a high-intensity combat zone," Kent told me in Sarajevo. "It started with the CNN factor — unsubstantiated media reports. Then the UN tried to avoid further political embarrassment instead of doing their job. If they had made a commitment to maintaining an open route for supplies to get into Mostar we wouldn't have had those problems on the Bosnian side. In East Mostar they thought this convoy would be a one-shot deal. By holding us there, they could try to insure the UN would make a real commitment to keep them from being starved to death.

"The people in Civil Affairs were divided among themselves," he said. "And the Spanish peacekeepers were answering two masters at once, the UN and Madrid. Once they overcame the HVO obstacles and made it to the Bosnian side, the peacekeepers forgot — or were ordered to forget — their military skills."

If the UN had followed standard principles of war and special operations, he believed, the relief effort would have gone off with fewer mishaps. "There's a certain amount of synergy that comes from putting together humanitarian and military efforts. The military has wonderful assets — convoy transportation, communications, and security — civilian agencies can use to keep supply routes open and deliver aid. And the military? Their lives are made much easier if they're seen as part of a humanitarian mission.

"Unfortunately," Kent said with a grin, "many humanitarians are jealous of their turf. They don't like to share it with the baby killers. And most world militaries are new to the doctrine of supporting peacekeeping and humanitarian efforts. It's really a matter of time. The civilian agencies and the military have to get used to working together."

Kent passed through a military checkpoint and parked the APC outside the building in which IRC had its offices and Egyptian peacekeepers barracked. "Here in Sarajevo, we let UN military observers distribute where they have access and we don't. They take our supplies, which earns them good will and gets our goods to remote areas." But this, according to Kent, was an exceptional situation. "Too many people in the UN are more interested in having their contract renewed at the end of three or six months than in solving the problem they've been sent to solve."

"People have needs beyond food and water," said Dana Rotberg, the Mexican filmmaker and co-organizer of the Sarajevo Film Festival. Ten days after my unexpected meeting with Kent Morris, I caught up with her in the London Café, which had just opened near the offices of IRC. A petite woman with short brown hair and large glasses, she smoked Marlboros, drained cup after cup of espresso, and spoke in a gravelly staccato. "In every city of the world people have the right to watch films," she said, explaining the genesis of the film festival. "Why not Sarajevo?"

I had come to the capital to cover this event. The siege of Sarajevo was now in its eighteenth month. Ten thousand people had lost their lives, including at least two thousand children. Tens of thousands more had been wounded, and hundreds of millions of dollars worth of damage had been inflicted on the city that had hosted the 1984 Winter Olympics—a multicultural, multi-confessional beacon of hope (or so it had seemed) in a sea of nationalist fury. From their positions in the mountains surrounding the city, the Bosnian Serbs rained down shells and snipers' bullets on civilians, routinely cut off the gas and electricity, and destroyed the water lines. For food Sarajevans relied on the airlift and the black market. It was a desperate situation.

To make matters worse, the people suffered from an insidious, war-inflicted boredom. Without electricity they could not watch television or videos, and there was no light to read by — assuming any books remained. The previous winter they had burned books, furniture, and most of the city's majestic trees to cook and to heat their houses and apartments. How to aesthetically and spiritually survive the Serbs' slow strangulation of Sarajevo was the question Rotberg and Haris Pašović, Bosnia's celebrated theater director, put to themselves. The film festival, titled Beyond the End of the World, was their answer. In ten days they showed more than one hundred films; it was usually standing room only in Radnik Theater, which holds 400 people, despite the efforts of a sniper who liked to make it "hot" by the entrance.

"Snipers are a technical problem for us," Dana said bitterly, "like trying to line up enough diesel to show a film."

These were hardly the only problems she and Pašović faced. The festival, sponsored by IRC, *Action Internationale Contre la Faim* (AICF), and the Soros Foundation, got off to a bad start. A nine-hour Serbian artillery attack on Sarajevo left ten people dead and scores wounded.

Meanwhile, at the airport in Ancona, Italy, where part of the airlift originated and UNHCR allowed journalists to board its flights, another drama was concluding. Vanessa Redgrave, Jeremy Irons, Daniel Day-Lewis, and six other luminaries from the film world had planned to attend the festival, in a show of solidarity. They were bringing new films to screen, including *The House of the Spirits* and *In the Name of the Father*. But the actors never made it to Sarajevo. UNHCR (backed up by Civil Affairs) refused to let them on a flight because they were neither journalists nor relief workers.

This was particularly galling to Redgrave. Despite an earlier visit to the city as a guest of UNICEF, a formal invitation from Rotberg and Pasović, press accreditation from the British Film Institute, and reporting assignments for her and her colleagues, she could not convince authorities to let them attend the festival. A series of phone calls to Cedric Thornberry's office, late into the night, came to nothing. The next morning it appeared, briefly, that one member of Redgrave's entourage, Terry George, a respected journalist and senior editor at *Travel Holiday,* might be allowed to go to Sarajevo. But that, too, was scuttled when UNHCR discovered he shared a screenwriting credit on *In the Name of the Father*—as a participant in Beyond the End of the World he could not write "an objective account of the proceedings," they said.

Before she and her colleagues boarded a charter jet to Munich, Redgrave vowed to return to Sarajevo. "They're saving us," she said of the people whose city was hit by more than 900 shells that day.

The festival went on without its distinguished guests. The event, though part of an effort to open a cultural corridor into the capital and help break the Serbian siege, received little attention from the media. But as Ademir Kenović, a filmmaker who has documented the destruction of his city in a series of powerful films, told me one day, "No one who sees even a single frame of the pictures from Sarajevo will ever rest easily. People everywhere are disturbed unconsciously by the siege; they know something horrible is happening. If 400,000 people are in concentration camps, with the cooperation of the political and moral zeroes on the world's stage, then it's obvious this cannot end up good for anybody."

Beyond the End of the World had a volunteer staff of eighty who worked around the clock, some staying up all night to subtitle videotapes (there was no projection equipment on which to screen prints), others printing daily schedules that were subject to constant change, and still others solving problems that would not occur in peacetime. Midway through the festival, for example, the Bosnian government ordered everyone to stay inside while special police units tracked down two renegade warlords. That day

52

there were firefights in the city. The next day there were films again.

"A civic attachment to life is a form of resistance," Rotberg maintained. "People here try to live normally in this abnormality. They can't defend themselves because of the arms embargo, they're shelled, they're massacred, yet they're determined to *live,* not just survive. And this festival is a way of breaking the siege. The films are a window onto the world. You see people running through the sniper fire, laughing, hiding behind cars, just to get to the cinema."

Rotberg, the acclaimed director of *Angel of Fire,* had moved to Sarajevo three months earlier, planning to make a film about the siege of the city. But to do that, she realized, "you have to live here and understand the texture of the people's lives. Otherwise it's just CNN reportage. So I thought, if I can't do a film, I'll bring a film festival to town."

I asked whether it was worth the trouble, the tremendous risks.

"One day we showed *Aladdin,*" she said, brightening. "Hundreds of kids who were only two years old when this stupid war started went for the first time to the cinema. If that doesn't justify a film festival, what does?

"People have needs beyond food and water," she repeated. "Going to the cinema *is* a kind of resistance. You can stay in your cellar, or you can go to a film. That's the point. This city is not in a cellar. That's why it's still alive."

But the siege of Sarajevo did not lift. The war raged on in Bosnia, the world averted its glance again, and two days after I flew home the Old Bridge in Mostar was destroyed.

Humanitarian space is crucial to alleviating suffering, according to Nicholas Morris, UNHCR Special Envoy to the former Yugoslavia. But in this war it is almost impossible to carve out space in which to safely deliver relief. In September 1994 Morris, a tall, lanky man with a clipped Australian accent, ushered me into his office in Zagreb to reflect on the problems UNHCR faced. Nearing the end of his assignment in the Balkans, the Special Envoy was candid about "the quagmire" into which the UN had sunk. Like other diplomats, journalists, and commentators, he believed it was time to rethink the role of humanitarian operations in war.

And no wonder. The nature of war itself had changed in the new world order. Clausewitz wrote that war was "the continuation of politics by other means"; the post-Cold War era, "a time of uncertainties," as some called it, was rife with unpredictable politics, whose "other means" now embraced ethnic skirmishes, religious terrorism, and intra- as opposed to interstate battles. The principal victims? Civilians, bystanders. Ninety-five percent of the casualties in World War I were military and 5 percent civilian; in World War II the numbers turned around—75 percent civilian, 25 percent military; and in Bosnia it was quite possible the World War I casualty percentages would be inverted. Add to that the millions of people displaced by the fighting and the growing reluctance of countries in the developed world to accept refugees, and the challenges facing humanitarians loomed ever larger. The UN designated 1994 as the International Year of the Family, in 1995 the world body celebrates its fiftieth anniversary — these shows of self-congratulation ring hollow in light of the Third Balkan War.

The humanitarian situation was steadily deteriorating. The month before, the Bosnian Army's Fifth Corps had liberated the Bihać pocket from Fikret Abdić, the Muslim businessman-turned-renegade warlord. This was the prelude to an autumn campaign in which government forces would net some ninety-five square miles of territory from Bosnian Serbs — only to be overrun two weeks later. The dramatic success of the Bosnian Serb counteroffensive (backed by rebel Muslims loyal to Abdić, Serbs from Krajina — the Serbian-occupied part of Croatia — and weaponry from the JNA), coupled with the failure of the UN and NATO to take decisive action, would poison relations among the Western powers. On a visit to Sarajevo, UN Secretary General Boutros Boutros-Ghali would be jeered at by an angry crowd bearing derisive placards like "Hitler-Ghali." NATO would draw up evacuation plans for the peacekeepers and relief workers. The third winter of war promised to be the worst yet.

Meanwhile, 30,000 Muslims loyal to Abdić had fled from the predominately Muslim Bosnian army into Krajina. Croatia no longer accepted refugees, particularly Muslims, so over half of Abdić's followers found shelter in a converted chicken farm owned by his food conglomerate. They lived in chicken coops, surrounded by Serbs who welcomed them only because they represented a rebuke to the Bosnian government. Elsewhere, in a two-day referendum the Bosnian Serbs rejected another international peace plan, the siege of Sarajevo intensified, and in northeastern Bosnia ethnic cleansing continued apace — with this difference: the Muslims in Janja and Bijeljina now had to *pay* the Serbs before they could leave — a "toll" of $100 each for old women and children, $1,000 for able-bodied males.

UNHCR was in a tough position. The problems, as Nicholas Morris saw it, stemmed from the fact that the agency was working for the first time in "a country of origin." The three-way conflict accentuated the hazards of preserving humanitarian space, which he said was "getting more and more eroded because nobody respects humanitarian principles. And the longer we try and do this, the more difficult it is finally to say this effort is impartial.

"Take the example of last winter, when the whole of

central Bosnia was surrounded by active front lines. Serbs around Sarajevo, or the fighting between Croats and Muslims. If central Bosnia survived, it was because an enormous humanitarian effort crossed these lines with international drivers. How do you convince the soldiers with their fingers on the triggers that this is a neutral act? They think we're feeding the enemy. Both [Mate] Boban, the Croat leader, and Karadžić would say the same thing: 'You want the war to end? Stop your humanitarian assistance.'"

Humanitarian space depends upon national interests — or self-interests — overlapping with humanitarian principles. But in this war there is no overlap at all, said Morris. "They [all three sides] don't see any self-interest in respecting our principles, because they don't perceive our operation as being impartial and neutral." While the Serbs and Croats believed UNHCR was helping the enemy, he said, the Muslims thought that if the international community hadn't let them down there wouldn't be a need for a humanitarian operation. "They say, 'You're here. We're not allowed to arm ourselves or we'd have dealt with this. Do your job. If we could defend ourselves, we'd keep these roads open, we wouldn't need your help.'" At the same time, forced to choose between humanitarian and political or military imperatives, in Morris's view the Muslims, like the Serbs and Croats, often chose the latter, even if that meant more suffering for their own civilians.

The question of impartiality may never be resolved. For although UNHCR obeyed humanitarian principles, its partner in this operation, UNPROFOR, had to answer to the UN Security Council — i.e., to political thinkers. When UNPROFOR escorted convoys through Bosnian Serb-controlled areas it was an arm of the humanitarian assistance operation, said Morris. "But this same UNPROFOR has NATO going round overhead. And if you call in close air support, or contemplate air strikes, or set ultimatums, you're the instrument of the international community. You can't be seen as neutral."

The relief effort, then, became politicized. "In an operation where every further step of our involvement was predicated on the international community finding a political settlement that would put the genies back in the bottle, and this never happened, we got further away from our principles. Mrs. [Sadako] Ogata [the UN High Commissioner for Refugees] said humanitarian assistance cannot be a substitute for the political will to address the causes that make it necessary. Keep the separation clear between humanitarian organizations, which have to work on all sides, and the political.

"What was the view in the main capitals about Bosnia?" he said. "Answer: We're supporting the humanitarian relief operation, plus whatever else happens to be the flavor of the month in terms of negotiations. *My* concern is that the international community will see UNHCR as a useful stopgap rather than an arm that needs to be protected. They'll say, 'Well, UNHCR served as a fig leaf for our inability to decide what to do about war in the Balkans. Let's try them again.'"

(One glaring example to support the Special Envoy's claim: Warren Zimmerman, former U.S. Ambassador to Yugoslavia, directed our refugee relief operation until January 1994. Asked to explain why he resigned that post, he replied, "I had reached the conclusion that the humanitarian element for which I was responsible was being used as a cover for the lack of a real policy toward Bosnia.")

What lessons could be drawn from the Bosnian debacle?

"At UNHCR we've learned lots of practical lessons," Morris said, "one being never to assume the will of the international community is going to be done. But the real lesson is a political one, which is starkly obvious: if you're going to take a stand where everyone would say there is a moral imperative, then difficult as it is you have to take it because it's going to get more difficult—and then it's going to be impossible.

"Governments were simply not prepared to face what should be done. The political will must be exercised while containment is still possible. It might have been very difficult, though that's debatable, at the beginning to take a firm stand. In Vukovar, for example. But no one is ever going to convince me that it would have been harder than trying to do something now."

And the refugees? "In the foreseeable future, which is pretty short in the Balkans, I see no prospects of refugees returning to areas in which they would be minorities. It may sound naïve to say it, but the creation of conditions — i.e., political progress and solutions — must precede the return of refugees. You can't put it the other way around and call it a pilot project of putting people back in the zone of separation when there's no progress towards a political resolution."

Frederick Cuny is a legendary name in humanitarian circles. Head of Intertect Relief and Reconstruction, a private consulting firm based in Dallas, he has been called "the Red Adair of disaster relief"— and has been accused of working for the CIA. In truth, Cuny is a former civil rights worker and a self-described activist Democrat, a prolific writer and a licensed pilot; he started out as a city planner but for more than twenty years he has organized relief efforts for victims of war, famine, and natural catastrophe. Intertect, renowned for its ability to act quickly, has provided technical assistance in more than sixty countries, including Armenia, Bangladesh, Ethiopia, Guatemala, Haiti, Kurdistan, Mexico, Nigeria, Sri Lanka, Sudan, Turkey, and Zaire. A brusque ex-Marine, Cuny has built a reputation for getting things done.

In Bosnia, that meant restoring water and natural gas to Sarajevo, developing a winterization program for houses and refugee centers, and repairing classrooms.

The construction of an emergency water treatment system for Sarajevo was a typical Intertect project. In the first days of the war the Serbs severed all the water lines into the city, leaving Sarajevans with only three sources of clean water — two small wells under the city's sole brewery and the Miljačka River. The Miljačka runs through the center of town and is, predictably, exposed to shell fire and sniping. (Nearly 80% of all casualties in the first year of the war occurred within 250 meters of either side of the river.) Thus in April 1993, Intertect and IRC contracted with a Houston engineering consortium to build five portable water treatment modules, which the U.S. military then shipped to Croatia. Loaded onto Canadian air force transport planes (with only inches to spare), they were flown into Sarajevo in August, at the rate of one per week. The airport was on the front line, in the sights of Serbian artillery, so the modules were pulled from the plane on wheels designed to be hooked up to a big-rig truck. In less than ten minutes they were on their way to a tunnel in the city, where they would be safe from shelling.

Cuny's local engineers and water experts had found on old civic maps a network of cisterns and channels which could be refilled and used to distribute water. Accordingly, the river was dammed above the ancient system, a pipeline and pumps delivered water to the modules, and purified water was then pumped to an abandoned reservoir under an Austro-Hungarian fortress eighty meters above the tunnel. By the new year Cuny's system was up and running. With the completion of a second system — housed in a tunnel carved through a mountain and made of bricks taken from destroyed buildings, steel rails from the train yard, cement, dirt, steel panels, and junk cars — at the nearby Moscanica stream, water could be supplied to 60 percent of the city.

In September 1994 I met Fred Cuny for breakfast at the Hotel Intercontinental in Zagreb, and while we talked Serbian gunners were shelling — to no avail — his water treatment system. The tall, husky Texan drew my attention to the most important development in disaster relief, the collapse of the Soviet Union.

"It used to be in any crisis everyone would take sides and even the most pissant little problem would get elevated into international importance," he said. "There were very few cases where East and West lined up on the same side, so it was hard for humanitarian agencies to cross lines and get in and help. They were leery of being seen as a party to the conflict. But now that our response has become needs-based as opposed to politically based, agencies are willing to take the kinds of risks necessary to save lives.

Now we realize we can solve a problem at its source."

During the Cold War, he said, "humanitarian aid was designed *not* to be more than superficial, otherwise you'd get into root causes. For example, why do earthquakes kill so many people? Because the poor don't have good land choices. They end up living in vulnerable areas — steep hillsides that slide, river bottom areas that flood. You come in with humanitarian aid, but what you need to do is to get the people to safer land. And you can't do that without addressing land reform issues, which during the Cold War tended to be captured by the Marxists. Everything was geared to a political as opposed to a humanitarian view of the world."

Future humanitarian responses, he predicted, would be affected by the fact that it is possible to look at the causes of disasters and wars in a more dispassionate light.

"In Bosnia, it's pretty clear the Serbs have been the aggressors. The same thing in Rwanda, where we know who did most of the massacring. What started a conflict will influence who should and shouldn't be helped."

The problem was that in the last decade the doctrine of strict neutrality had taken the place of national sovereignty as an excuse for not helping disaster victims. Bosnia was a good example of that doctrine corrupting humanitarian agencies and international institutions. It was a matter of telling the truth, Cuny insisted. "For us to go in and not speak out against human rights abuses and gross violations of humanitarian principles is ridiculous. It's not worth the price of being able to get things in."

But in the wake of the Gulf War the intervention on behalf of the Kurds had introduced the principle that victims have rights to international aid. "It isn't codified yet," he said, "but it's coming. As long as there's no major bipolar confrontation with both sides squaring off and using conflicts as proxy wars, we have a chance of establishing the principle of going in and resolving issues peacefully, or by using force, if necessary."

Cuny wanted to redefine refugees to include anyone displaced by conflict, and then expand UNHCR to become an activist agency. A UN High Commissioner for War Victims, if you will. Only then could we "start dealing with something the moment it happens. We've got to get beyond this idea of strict neutrality. We've got to say, if people are in harm's way, we've got to get them out of there. The first and most important thing is saving lives. Whatever it takes to save lives, you do it, and the hell with national sovereignty. There's a higher responsibility: get the people out of harm's way, then deal with the other issues. It may mean you evacuate them to safe areas in their own country. Or request military assistance to create a safe area. Or provide food through the back door, if a government cuts its own people off. It has to be a proactive agency—you can't wait for victims to come to your door. Go out and deal with the problem when it starts."

This would require decisive action from the State Department, which could create an office of humanitarian crisis management, uniting political, humanitarian, and peacekeeping functions. "We have to get our house in order," said Cuny, "and merge these three issues. We need to project humanitarian assistance in the same way that the military projects power. If we can do that, we can go to the UN and say, this is how we want you to do it."

The prevailing policy has to change, as the war in Bosnia has made plain. "The UN's presence has certainly helped keep access open for humanitarian goods. We've been able to do airdrops and get supplies in on the airlift. Have we had success? In a limited way. Nobody's dying of lack of food, they're dying because of bullets." The real story was "the tremendous failure of all the collective security arrangements"—of the UN Security Council, UNPROFOR, NATO, CSCE, and the European Community. And the result?

"Some people think it's the death of the EC," he said. "I think it's the death of the European spirit of doing anything outside of what's traditionally thought of as Europe. It could mark the resurgence of ultranationalism based on ethnic or religious definitions. I worry about the future of Europe because of its failure to do anything in Bosnia."

I could not imagine him worrying for long. Activism and accountability were his watchwords. Tragedy aside, a disaster, he liked to say, was also an opportunity: "If we throw junk aid at a problem, there won't be any impact, even if it might soothe someone's conscience, especially donors." For example, he recommended buying land after an earthquake; when the rich sell it off to get enough money to rebuild their industries, there is a chance to move the poor onto good land.

"Start with something you can really do," he said. "Many agencies want to give them tents. That doesn't solve the problem. Give them tools and let them salvage what they can from the fallen buildings. Ninety percent is reusable. You let them take the bricks and steel and wood, put in some materials to help them build components, and you've begun reconstruction. If you just give people a tent, what does that tell them? Either you don't want them on that land or this isn't the solution. You slow down reconstruction and create expectations you can't meet. But if you give them a tool kit and some basic materials the message is, Get on with it. Let's get this thing over with. Let's rebuild the community."

In Sarajevo his self-help initiatives, implemented by IRC, took a different form: In the first winter of the siege, city residents were encouraged to tap into the natural gas line running from Russia. IRC imported thirty thousand meters of plastic pipe, promising it to any neighborhood willing to dig trenches in which to bury it, and then taught people how to tap into the line; the Serbs, who also needed the natural gas, would not completely shut it off. In the spring, Cuny and others encouraged IRC to bring in a thousand tons of seeds for backyard and balcony gardens; by late summer, fresh produce was in the market and Sarajevans were laying in preserves and canned vegetables for the winter.

"The first line of defense in famine and conflicts," he said, "is to get the markets going."

He praised IRC for employing city residents to manufacture beds and bedrolls for refugee centers — anything to pump money into the economy instead of buying goods overseas (though many agencies are hampered by governmental policies requiring them to purchase goods in donor countries). He even saw some merit in trading with the enemy, hence his grudging approval of the black market, which was responsible for bringing in resources — cigarettes, liquor, fresh produce — the UN could not supply. "Up to a point, every time you trade across lines you break those lines down."

"And I'm not naïve about corruption," he said, grinning. "I come from Texas, the most corrupt state in the Union, with the possible exception of Louisiana — and I grew up in Louisiana! In every war zone you expect to deal with corrupt militia and politicians and gangs. In this war it's clear the Bosnians, for all their faults, are the good guys. Their cause is worth fighting for unless they completely surrender to the mafias. They haven't done that yet."

Cuny would know, having suffered repeated delays in securing permission to run the water treatment system. Some government officials had blackmailed IRC by refusing to declare the water clean unless the NGO added several hundred thousand dollars' worth of equipment for the system, all to be purchased in Bosnia.

"You just keep fighting them," he said.

Ideally, humanitarians could help combat corruption, in the same way that they serve as witnesses against human rights abuses. Wherever humanitarian agencies expand their presence, he contended, there are fewer human rights abuses. In Banja Luka, for example, where Serbian forces were waging an intense campaign of ethnic cleansing against the Muslims, one UNHCR representative came up with an ingenious plan to stop some of the roundups. In his white UN vehicle he would follow suspicious cars heading into Bosnian neighborhoods. Risking his own life, he would park his car and go to the house he thought was targeted. "The Serbs wouldn't know why he was there," said Cuny, "and they'd leave."

But this was the work of an unusually dedicated individual. In most Serb-held areas UNHCR made little effort to protect civilians, though this was one of its missions. (The others were to provide humanitarian aid to displaced persons and refugees, then help them return to their homes.) In Cuny's view UNHCR had never developed a comprehensive humanitarian strategy, despite having lobbied to be the lead agency in this crisis. So much more could have been done.

"At the beginning of the war, when the Serbs didn't know what they could get away with, UNHCR could have gone to those places where Muslims were being attacked and made their presence felt. Bring in their own people. Deputize NGOs. Get bodies there to report on what was happening. We know increasing the presence of humanitarians dampens human rights abuses.

"But they didn't do it," he complained. "Every strategy you use to protect people, they ignored. They absolved themselves of any responsibility — without coming up with a plan of their own. They should have said, 'The way we've done business in a country of asylum is not going to work in Bosnia. So what do we do?' But they just settled into a comfortable routine here in Zagreb. They said it was too dangerous. I say they were so worried about their own staff they didn't worry enough about the victims. If you're going to save people, you have to take some risks."

"But what about their lack of support from the international community?" I asked.

"We design our operations on the assumption that there won't be international support," he replied. "We never expect it. We're surprised when there *is* intervention. We'd hope to see NATO come in and rescue Bosnia. But if they don't, that doesn't mean you stick your feet in the air and look like a dead cat. You make your own opportunities."

In the end it was a matter of accountability, at every level. UNHCR, human rights observers, humanitarian agencies, the media, all had a role to play in ensuring that the parties responsible for war atrocities knew the international community was watching them.

"Use the radio and flyers, deliver protests to the mayors of these towns, whatever it takes. Make them accountable," he said.

Cuny did not believe the War Crimes Tribunal would amount to much, even though thousands of pages of evidence documenting crimes against humanity have been collected and sent to the Hague. So he had another idea: publish the names of all the war criminals in their villages and cities. This would not bring back the dead, of course, nor would it offer justice to the rape victims. But it would make a statement and set a precedent for future conflicts. Shame is a powerful weapon. If nothing else, Cuny said, the war criminals' wives and neighbors would know what they had done. "And nobody wants their children to know they were rapists."

I wondered how the Serbs, who had so shamed themselves in this war, might be reintegrated into the international community. Cuny thought Serbia would become a pariah, like Iran. "The destruction of Vukovar and Sarajevo will not be forgiven the Serbs," wrote the American poet Charles Simic, who before the war had translated a number of Serbian poets and promoted their work in this country.

> Whatever moral credit they had as a result of their history they have squandered in these two acts. The suicidal and abysmal idiocy of nationalism is revealed here better than anywhere else. No human being or group has the right to pass a death sentence on a city.

> "Defend your own, but respect what others have," my grandfather used to say, and he was a highly decorated officer in the First World War and certainly a Serbian patriot. I imagine he would have agreed with me. There will be no happy future for people who have made the innocent suffer.

And the danger, according to Cuny, was that the Serbs might come out of the war believing themselves to be victims of the West, making the region even more unstable. Like Germany, which after World War II attempted to purge itself of Nazism and reckon with its crimes, Serbia must come to terms with what it has wrought in Croatia and Bosnia. It must do some soul searching, he said.

"It doesn't look like that will happen, though," I said.

"It's not over yet," Cuny said. "If the war goes on too long, they'll pay a price as well."

I was inclined to believe him. On one trip to Sarajevo I had read Intertect's briefing book on Bosnia, a reference work on the humanitarian and military situations. Impressed with the accuracy of Cuny's predictions about the progress of the war, I had always wanted to ask him what his secret was. He replied with a story. "One of my flying buddies is an instructor on Lear jets. He told me about a scenario on the simulator where the pilots, especially the experienced ones, kept flying the plane into the ground. They couldn't figure out why. They looked at cause and effect and why people make certain decisions. They looked at real cases. Then they fed all this information — everything from power settings to weather briefings — into the training program. Sure enough, the experienced pilots kept crashing. Why?

"Well, they realized the problem was the weather briefing. In every accident it said the weather at the destination would be better than it was. They weren't mentally prepared for the worst-case scenario. They thought the cloud ceiling would be 700 [feet] broken, but the weather had changed and now it was 300. As they went down to decision height, where you're guaranteed obstruction clearance, they kept expecting to break out of the clouds. So they pushed a little lower and a little lower. Next thing you know, *Boom*. They were in the ground. The same scenario applies to disaster relief, and to disastrous decisions made at the top.

"There's someone at the UN who should be prosecuted as a war criminal," Cuny argued, his voice rising. "Twice in the past he delayed making critical decisions, and thousands of people died. I went to him and said, 'Look, the first time I understand why you didn't act. But the second time the same thing happened, and you delayed making decisions until it was too late. Why?' He said, 'I always figured if things got really bad the West was going to come in with a massive humanitarian airlift.'

"My God, do you know how much it costs to airlift enough food to feed 500,000 people? I actually sat down with this man and worked it out. He said, 'No wonder they didn't do it.' But he was always blaming the international community for not coming to his rescue. He expected a certain outcome, which led him to take risks, because like too many people he had this idea from the news media and the history of relief operations that in a big crisis the cavalry was going to come. It rarely happens.

"In disasters these same people expect a certain outcome, and then things change, and they're too slow to adapt. Next thing you know they've got a major problem on their hands. Last summer UNHCR was convinced the Serbs would accept the Vance-Owen peace plan, so they quit preparing for the winter. They coasted through the whole debate, and suddenly the plan was dead. They didn't have enough food and no winterization program. Typical situation — they always choose the optimistic scenario.

"What we've got to do," he said, "is focus on how you teach a decision maker what his options are and when to act. You have to explain that the longer you delay making decisions, the more the chance of making good ones declines. It goes from being a good choice to a bad choice to no choice."

By the fall of 1994 there were few choices left in Bosnia. When Germany had first prepared to recognize Slovenia and Croatia, Cuny suggested, the international community had its best chance to act, and it failed. "One thing I've learned about dictators," he said with a smile, "is most of them are cowards. They may be bullies, but they won't surrender their power unless threatened by an overwhelming force. There were times when our threats, if they were credible, would have been enough. To get the high ground back now will require a lot more force.

"And the question goes beyond containment when it comes to Kosovo." Serbia's southern province, 90 percent Albanian and suffering repression by the Serbs, was, in the words of one diplomat, "a massacre waiting to happen": Milošević was believed to have designs on Kosovo, and it was said the JNA could overrun the province in forty-eight hours. Some observers called Kosovo "Europe's dirty little secret": the Serbs were openly practicing apartheid against the Albanians — and no one was stopping them. "Kosovo is dangerous," Cuny said, "because it involves Albania and Macedonia, Bulgaria and Turkey, and of course Greece. It's the fault line between the Orthodox and Muslim worlds. And it ignites all the old Balkan questions. You've really got to stomp it out. It's not going to burn out on its own."

His thoughts shifted back to the present conflict. "The real tragedy of Bosnia," he said, "is that the best people are leaving. The young people, the innovative ones who would be the real heart of the country, see no future there. They're giving up on the idea of Bosnia. And any hope of a viable country remaining after this war is rapidly evaporating. So the Serbs have won an immoral victory."

He signaled for the check. He was on his way to Berlin to discuss a new Carnegie Endowment report on the Third Balkan War. The recent republication of the Endowment's report on the first two Balkan Wars had inspired George Kennan to draw conclusions about the current war. After noting many similarities in the behavior of the combatants in all three wars, Kennan set two requirements for those on the "outside" seeking to end the conflict: "One will be a capacity for innovation with respect to the rights and duties implicit in the term 'sovereignty.' The other will be force — minimum force, of course, but force nevertheless — and the readiness to employ it where nothing else will do." Humanitarians like Frederick Cuny were already meeting Kennan's first requirement. The second was a story to save for another day.

I traveled to Mostar in September 1994, the same week Pope John Paul II intended to visit Sarajevo and Zagreb. Indeed it was the Pontiff's journey that convinced me to go to Mostar instead of Sarajevo; journalists from around the world were planning to cover his trip, and I did not want to wait with them in Ancona, Italy, hoping to find a place on a UNHCR flight to Sarajevo. Late one afternoon in Zagreb I boarded a bus to Mostar, mindful of the botched relief operation Kent Morris had told me about. Mindful, too, of the destruction of the Old Bridge the previous November, an act which had taken on enormous significance: in this war nothing was sacrosanct. The Croatian writer Slavenka Drakulić asked:

> Finally — who did it? The Muslims are accusing the Croats, the Croats are accusing the Muslims. But does it even matter? For four centuries people needed that bridge and admired its beauty. The

question is not who shelled and demolished it. The question is not even why someone did it — destruction is part of human nature. The question is: What kind of people do not need that bridge. The only answer I can come up with is this: people who do not believe in the future — theirs or their children's — do not need such a bridge.

Despite the enmity between Bosnia and Croatia, the barbaric acts committed by their armies, and more senseless destruction of private property, religious sites, and cultural monuments, in March 1994 the Presidents of Bosnia and Croatia, Alija Izetbegović and Franjo Tudjman, flew to Washington to sign the U.S.-brokered Bosniak-Croat federal agreement, pledging to work together to reverse "ethnically defined politics." For three years, ombudsmen — one Bosniak, one Croat, and one "other" — appointed by the CSCE would serve with wide-ranging powers to protect human rights in the new federation.

"We have seen the light at the end of the tunnel," said Bosnia's UN Ambassador Mohamed Sacirbey. "We don't know yet where it will lead us exactly, but it is a light and we are following it."

In Mostar I hoped to glimpse that light; however, Nicholas Morris's words seemed closer to the mark. "For the Croats the Federation was an imposed marriage. That's not *Balkan*," UNHCR's Special Envoy had told me. "For the Bosniaks it was an arranged marriage, with mother or mother-in-law being in Washington — that's very Balkan, but not necessarily durable."

The bus made an unscheduled stop in the middle of the night in the mountains outside Zadar, Croatia, when the generator failed. The driver pulled over to the side of the road, tried for an hour to fix the generator, then advised us to get some sleep. "Not a good place to park," said a British journalist sitting across from me, a man who had reported from the Balkans for more than fifteen years. We were an easy target for any Serbs who might have occupied the ridge above us. I wished I did not have a window seat.

But no shots were fired, and at five in the morning we resumed our journey. Through the lingering darkness we drove without lights. By daybreak we were barreling along the Dalmatian coast, the sea glittering in the distance. At the border the guards closely questioned an old woman who we knew was smuggling shirts; three large duffel bags covered with meshing, which may have been filled with guns and grenades, were not examined. The mood lightened once we were in Herzegovina.

"They're going home," the British journalist said of our fellow passengers, some of whom were returning refugees. Later, as we drove down the winding mountain road toward Mostar, he pointed to the medieval city nestled in the Neretva River valley. "It looks so peaceful," he said softly. "You would never guess they've been slaughtering one another for three years now."

A Croatian woman, a friend who had worked in Mostar as a journalist during the worst of the fighting between the Croats and Bosnians, had suggested I stay in the Franciscan monastery. When the bus let us out in the western half of the city (a banner hanging above the street read, *Dobro Došli u Hrvatski Mostar*—"Welcome to Croatian Mostar"), I walked to the monastery, which was located on the front line. The church itself was destroyed; the long thin logs propped against the back wall marked the front line. I saw three policemen in shirtsleeves sitting at a table, drinking beer, and then I heard the blast of a grenade: unexploded ordnance set off in a dumpster adjacent to the church. One policeman led me down a set of stairs protected by logs blackened in a fire into the basement of the monastery, where two monks in work clothes were finishing lunch.

My friend had not succeeded in contacting the monks she knew; they were on their way to Zagreb. To see the Pontiff in Sarajevo would have meant far less travel, and although such a journey was fraught with danger, its symbolic value would have been immense. But the Franciscans preferred to be in Croatia: anti-Muslim feelings were running high on this side of the city. The monks in the basement were guarding what was left of their monastery.

Little remained intact. Most of the cells were damaged, the red-tile roof was covered with holes, the library was destroyed; walls were propped up with sandbags; and in the courtyard, where forty grenades had landed, a charred cross with the plastic date 1992 nailed across it was surrounded by palms and roses. The monks showed me a room the size of a walk-in closet, now used for Mass. They sadly shook their heads. There was no place for me to stay. As I was leaving, one monk gave me a postcard displaying photographs of the church taken before and after the fighting.

"Crazy," he said.

I went to the Hotel Ero, where the European Union (EU) had opened offices, establishing a provisional government under the leadership of Hans Koschnick, the former mayor of Cologne. A young Croatian woman working for the EU rented me an abandoned flat for thirty-five dollars per night. The owners, she said, were not coming back. I could stay as long as I liked. Three Italians, two young men and an older woman separated from a Catholic group driving to Sarajevo, swept into the hotel, needing directions to the capital. They *had* to see the Pope, they told the Croatian woman repeatedly. Their idealism was touching, their naïveté frightening.

Once installed in my flat, I spent much of the day walking around West Mostar, inspecting the damage. There were houses, apartments, and municipal buildings destroyed by artillery fire or dynamite; a shelled stadium and shrapnel-pocked walls; streets gouged by grenades and missiles. The traffic lights did not work, and cars careened around intersections, honking their horns at white UN and EU vehicles. Serbian forces were behind one mountain range, Croats behind the other. "The Serbs could shoot at us at any time," said the Croatian bartender who served me a beer late in the afternoon. In the early evening I walked to the bread factory overlooking the river. There I met and spoke with two Croatian special policemen who only months before had been soldiers fighting in the Croatian Army.

"This is a Disney war," one said enigmatically. "You can rent a tank over there. I don't think it's a good idea to give the Muslims arms, but we're giving them everything—arms, food, clothes."

Then he proceeded to show off his own equipment, most of which—his new uniform, his knife, his radio with twenty bands on which we listened to Serb and Muslim fighters trade insults and threats—came from America. Only his pistol was manufactured in Croatia, as it said, in English, on the handle: MADE IN CROATIA.

The other policeman pointed to the former JNA

barracks on the other side of the river, less than one hundred meters away, where Muslim forces were now housed. "You see that building? Those houses? They're filled with gold. Many people got rich off this war. We will never get along," he confided. "We're too different, maybe because of our religion."

"What do you think of the Pope going to Sarajevo?" I asked.

They shook their heads. "I have a bad feeling," said the first policeman. "We listen to the Serbs and Muslims on the radio, and both sides hate the Pope. There are lots of people who would like to go down in history as the one who killed the Pope — they're the only criminals anyone remembers, like Oswald or O.J. Simpson. And these guys have Strelas [surface-to-air missiles]!"

On either bank of the river teenaged boys in bathing suits were fishing and throwing rocks into the water, cheerfully calling one another names — the Croats were Ustaše, the Muslims, Titoists.

"The Muslims didn't arm themselves," said the first policeman. "They thought the West would save them. You see what they did to us? Nothing compared to what we did to them. We flattened their buildings, they just threw crap at us. But the Serbs did the real damage," he said with a touch of awe.

"Who blew up the Old Bridge?" I said.

"The Muslims care more for bridges than for people," the first policeman sneered.

"It was an old bridge, like an old person. It was time for it to die," said the second policeman. "Who blew it up? We did, they did, but we finished it off," he said proudly.

Early the next morning I went to the EU to get permission to go to East Mostar — a lengthy ordeal, although my press credentials were in order. I talked with a Spanish peace-keeper while I waited for the necessary paperwork to be processed. "I know every city and village in Bosnia," he said, describing his tour of duty, which was now in its twenty-first month. "I lived here in 1982. I never imagined they would fight like this. These people are crazy. Three sides, each fiercely hating the others."

When the paperwork was complete, I hurried across a temporary bridge replacing one of the city's five destroyed bridges. What a change from West Mostar where, the night before, the cafés and bars had been crowded, shops and kiosks filled with goods; there was even a carwash operating. In East Mostar, rows of lockers stuffed with bricks and debris lined the streets; men and women waited by spigots or water trucks to fill their plastic containers; sixteen thousand buildings and flats had been damaged or destroyed. Nothing had been spared, and there was no sign of gold in any house I entered. Although a poster bearing a plea to drive slowly now partly covered a sign warning of snipers, the graffiti around town told a different story. On the strafed walls of many buildings were the names of children killed in the war: *Saša, Ana, Hara.*

Green Islamic flags hung from balconies and above the streets. In a new graveyard, where there were scores of fresh graves and holes already dug for the next wave of casualties, all the wooden markers featured the same insignia, a star within a crescent moon; the damaged mosques were filled with old men and boys. The European fear that Islamic Fundamentalism would take hold in Bosnia, which had until now seemed farfetched, was becoming, day by day, a reality in East Mostar — one more blow to moderate and secular Muslims around the world already hard-pressed to explain to Muslim extremists and their followers the West's inaction in Bosnia.

In the Koski, Mehmed Paša's riverside mosque built in 1648 and all but obliterated last year, I met with Jadran Jelin, the man in charge of reconstructing Mostar. A former professor of civil engineering at the University of Mostar, he had spent ten months in a Croatian concentration camp, where the guards had once been his students. But he remembered also another Croatian student of his who had helped him move his belongings out of his flat in West Mostar before the HVO blew it up.

"There are still good people here in Mostar," Jelin insisted. "They'll rebuild this city. The Old Bridge will be rebuilt by the people of Mostar, just as it was in the sixteenth century.

"Everything is badly damaged. All the cultural monuments, mosques, and churches were destroyed, and the whole infrastructure — water and electricity — was demolished. We expect help from Europe and America. And we propose joint reconstruction with the European Union. *Their* first task is to connect both sides of the city."

I asked him about the fate of the Bosniak-Croat Federation. The stories I had heard in West Mostar, which now regarded itself as the capital of the separate state of Herzeg-Bosna, and the divisions I felt between the two sides of the city, the mutual suspicion and grief built up during the war, led me to doubt the enduring viability of this agreement. Two old women in East Mostar who had invited me in for a glass of juice expressed what seemed to be a common Muslim sentiment: they could probably live with the Serbs, they said, but not the Croats. Not after what the HVO had done to their side of the city. Moreover, in the Balkans there was no Abraham Lincoln composing a Gettysburg Address for Sarajevo or Mostar — no political figure, that is, capable of healing wounds and reuniting warring factions; much of the intellectual elite in places like Mostar had long ago fled to other countries.

"You have been listening to evil people," said Jelin. "We are good people. The peace will hold."

I wandered through the streets of East Mostar, past hundreds of gutted buildings, and crossed the makeshift bridge of wooden planks and cables that had replaced the Old Bridge. The Pope had decided not to go to Sarajevo. Bosnian Serb leader Radovan Karadžić warned he could not guarantee the Pontiff's safety. The Orthodox Church in Belgrade had already barred John Paul II's visit to Serbia. The religious figure that future historians will associate with the downfall of Communism had met his match in these nationalists. A sad day for the world, I was thinking, when I chanced upon a burned-out flat in which a Muslim artist was painting, his subject each time the Old Bridge, his charred walls covered with images of what had been. Not once did the young man look up from his canvas as I walked around the darkened room, studying his primitive renderings of the bridge constructed—legend has it—of mortar mixed with egg whites. There were no prices on his work. He had no interest in talking to me.

I went out into the sunshine. It was warm, a perfect Indian-summer day, and yet I was shivering. "The bridge," declares Slavenka Drakulić, "in all its beauty and grace, was built to outlive us. It was an attempt to grasp eternity.

Because it was the product of both individual creativity and collective experience, it transcended our individual destiny. A dead woman is one of us — but the bridge is all of us, forever." The artist in his dark flat was determined to preserve some vision of that eternity.

I walked up to three Bosnian policemen lounging by a pile of rubble; the front was only fifty meters away, they said, directing me toward a row of buildings behind which it was safe to walk. There I found the British journalist I had met on the bus. He was in Mostar on behalf of a German organization that wanted to build a community center here. Where to house such a center, in East or West Mostar, was what he had to decide. This flattened Muslim part of West Mostar seemed to be the best place.

Pointing at the rubble, he said, "This is the real crime. Here you can see the true horror of this war."

Indeed. Last winter some observers had noted the irony of the Holocaust Museum opening in Washington, D.C., its message — "Never again" — declared boldly even as genocide was being carried out again, this time in Bosnia. Here was indisputable evidence of our failure to act against aggression. Yet this was where the international community could have made a difference, the British journalist said, looking at the gutted buildings. "Your president," he said to me, "should have told the Croats, 'Look, you will not be part of Europe for the next twenty years if you don't stop shooting right now.' That wouldn't work with the Serbs, because they're not interested in Europe. But the Croats had something to lose. They want to belong to the West. Clinton let them get away with this. Should be enough to cost him the next election, don't you think?"

We walked on. Where the Marshal Tito Bridge had once stretched across the river, British peacekeepers were in the last stages of assembling a temporary replacement. Barbed wire was coiled around the construction site, cranes lifted girders on either side of the Neretva. In three days these troops had built a bridge big enough to handle trucks filled with food and other humanitarian supplies. We watched them lay a long green girder across the river.

"This is just practice for another Falklands," the journalist said bitterly. "The British army has thousands of these bridges lying around." But then he smiled. "What if we were to build our community center in three days? It could be done, couldn't it?"

That night I lay in the dark, in my flat, thinking about the wobbly cableway that took the place of the Old Bridge. Walking across it earlier, I kept losing my balance, especially when the Bosnian boys dove from it into the river some twenty meters below — a tradition their ancestors had practiced for hundreds of years from the Old Bridge. I reached for the cables, embarrassed by my clumsiness and afraid of falling. I stood there for a while as old men and women crossed without a flinch. It occurred to me that this is how connections are re-established between warring sides: with a makeshift bridge, which in turn will be replaced by a permanent structure. Eventually, the Europeans will close their offices in the Hotel Ero and leave. The people of East and West Mostar will have to find ways to live together.

I recalled a conversation from the year before. I had traveled to Dubrovnik, the medieval city on the Dalmatian coast that had suffered a three-month-long siege, its beautiful walls and streets relentlessly bombarded by the JNA. There I met an EC military monitor, who impressed me as a wise and humane man. In fifty years, he predicted, there will be another Yugoslavia.

"They'll have to live together, won't they?" he said.

I told him about a schoolteacher I knew from Vukovar, a young Croatian woman who was quarreling with her aunts because they had traded Christmas cards with Serbian women living in refugee centers in Belgrade. The schoolteacher could not understand why the older women would reach out to their enemies.

"Those Christmas cards are the best way to the future," said the monitor. "Lasting peace will come only with small gestures."

Bridges are built with such gestures. Imagine the

courage of the first ones to cross any bridge; in time whole generations will pass over it without firsthand knowledge of the terror preceding its construction. And humanitarians, to use a metaphor, are in the business of building bridges (in the same way that metaphor bridges disparate realms of experience). I took one step on this bridge. Another. I heard the shrieks of delight of children swimming and sunbathing below, and then just the wind.

Dedicated to Frederick Cuny

Disappeared in Chechnya
April 1995

*Action Internationale Contre la Faim* (AICF):
    French relief agency
Abdić, Fikret:
    Muslim businessman and renegade warlord
Boban, Mate:
    Leader of the Bosnian Croats
Boutros-Ghali, Boutros:
    UN Secretary General
Catholic Relief Services (CRS):
    American relief agency
Conference on Security and Cooperation in Europe (CSCE)
Croatian Defense Council (HVO):
    Croatian nationalist militia
European Union (EU), formerly known as the European
    Community (EC)
Gligorov, Kiro:
    President of Macedonia
Herzeg-Bosna:
    Self-proclaimed Bosnian Croat state

International Committee of the Red Cross (ICRC)
International Monetary Fund (IMF)
International Rescue Committee (IRC)
Intertect Relief and Reconstruction:
    American disaster relief consulting firm run by
    Frederick Cuny
Izetbegović, Alija:
    President of Bosnia-Herzegovina
Karadžić, Radovan:
    President of the Bosnian Serb Parliament
*Mèdecins Sans Frontières* (MSF):
    French relief agency
Milošević, Slobodan:
    President of Serbia
Nongovernmental organization (NGO)
North Atlantic Treaty Organization (NATO)
Ogata, Sadako:
    UN High Commissioner for Refugees
Open Society Institute/Soros Foundation:
    Humanitarian organizations funded by George Soros
Owen, Lord David:
    European Community Special Envoy to the former
    Yugoslavia
Pašović, Haris:
    Bosnian theater director and codirector of the Sarajevo
    Film Festival

Pavelić, Ante:
    Ustaša leader
Serbian Republic of Bosnia-Herzegovina:
    Self-proclaimed Bosnian Serb state
Soros, George:
    International financier
Thornberry, Cedric:
    Head of UNPROFOR Civil Affairs
Tito, Marshal (Josip Broz):
    Premier of Yugoslavia, 1945–1953
    President of Yugoslavia, 1953–1980
Tudjman, Franjo:
    President of Croatia
United Nations High Commissioner for Refugees
    (UNHCR)
United Nations International Children's Emergency
    Foundation (UNICEF)
United Nations Protection Forces (UNPROFOR)
Ustaša: Croatian Fascist regime (1941–45)
Vance, Cyrus:
    UN Special Envoy to the former Yugoslavia
World Food Programme (WFP)
World Health Organisation (WHO)
Yugoslav National Army (JNA)

Christopher Merrill is the author of three collections of poetry, *Workbook, Fevers & Tides,* and *Watch Fire;* editor of *Outcroppings: John McPhee in the West, The Forgotten Language: Contemporary Poets and Nature,* and (with Ellen Bradbury) *From the Faraway Nearby: Georgia O'Keeffe as Icon;* and translator (with the author) of Aleš Debeljak's *Anxious Moments.* His nonfiction books include *The Grass of Another Country: A Journey Through the World of Soccer* and a forthcoming work on the war in Bosnia, *Only the Nails Remain.* A freelance journalist, he lives in Portland, Oregon, with his wife, violinist Lisa Gowdy-Merrill.

Interior designed by Will Powers
Typeset in the Minion family
by Stanton Publication Services, Inc.
Printed on acid-free 55-pound Booktext Natural paper
by BookCrafters

MORE FROM THE MILKWEED EDITIONS
THISTLE SERIES:

*Bad Government and Silly Literature*
Carol Bly

*Rooms in the House of Stone*
Michael Dorris

*The Mythic Family*
Judith Guest

*I Won't Learn from You!*
*The Role of Assent in Learning*
Herbert Kohl

*A Male Grief*
*Notes on Pornography and Addiction*
David Mura

*What Makes Pornography "Sexy"?*
John Stoltenberg